FIELDNOTES

ON

ALLYSHIP

Our Human Family, Inc., Orlando
ourhumanfamily.org

Library of Congress Control Number: 2020917863

ISBN-13: 978-0-578-76750-5

PRINTED IN THE UNITED STATES OF AMERICA

30 29 28 27 26 25 24 23 22 21 20   1 2 3 4 5

Book and cover design by Clay Rivers

First Edition

FIELDNOTES

ON

ALLYSHIP

ACHIEVING EQUALITY TOGETHER

edited by
Clay Rivers
Sherry Kappel
Stephen Matlock

OUR HUMAN FAMILY, INC.
orlando
2020

For George

Breonna

Ahmaud

Jordan

Philando

Sandra

the Mother Emanuel Nine

Tamir

Michael

Eric

Trayvon

If we all are to be free,
then we all need to be allies in support
of the liberation of us all.

—JOEL LEON

CONTENTS

CONTENTS

FOREWORD

CLAY RIVERS

SUMMER 2020, PEOPLE THE world over learned the United States' ugly secret known by Black people in this country for 400 years: Black lives are regarded as having little to no value. And for any Black person who dares challenge this worldview, retribution can be sure, swift, and deadly.

In 1919, fifty-four years after the abolition of the enslavement of Black Americans and thirty-nine years after Black men were granted the right to vote, July Perry led a voter registration campaign for the Black residents of Ocoee, Florida. In response, white residents lynched him, ran all of the Black residents out of town, and burned their homes, churches, businesses, and farmland to the ground. No Black person voted again in Ocoee for at least fifty years.

In 1955, fourteen-year-old Emmett Till was brutally murdered for allegedly flirting with a white woman. Two men kidnapped the boy, beat and mutilated him, shot him in the head, tied a seventy-pound fan around his neck with barbed wire, and dumped his body in a nearby river. His body was found three days later. After an hour of deliberations, Till's murderers were acquitted by an all-white jury. Three months later, they confessed to the murder in a national magazine interview. Decades later, Till's accuser admitted she fabricated parts of her testimony.

As late as August 22, 2020, Trayford Pellerin was fatally shot outside a convenience store in Lafayette, Louisianna. The following day, Jacob Blake was shot in the back numerous times at close range in Kenosha, Wisconsin. Lest you think these horrors are one-offs or a freak occurrence, the National Museum for Peace and Justice in Montgomery, Alabama, memorializes close to 4,400 known victims of terror lynchings that occurred between 1877 and 1950. These events were not the exception, but the rule that governed the lives of Black people in America. This unspoken code of inequity continues up to the present day, as felt in the deaths of our fallen brothers and sisters Trayvon Martin, Eric Garner, Michael Brown, Tamir Rice, the Mother Emanuel Nine, Sandra Bland, Philando Castile, Jordan Edwards, Ahmaud Arbery, Breonna Taylor, George Floyd, and others too many to name.

These tragedies are emblematic of the Black experience

in America. The stone-cold nonchalance and frequency with which these acts of anti-Black hatred occur never cease to shake decent people to our core. We suppress the outrage over the innumerable indignities and microaggressions we endure for fear that revealing a sliver of our genuine frustration will only validate the angry Black person trope, land us in jail, or worse. We unflinchingly swim against the torrent of scorn and denigration, designed to rob us of our humanity and self-esteem. And we mask the grief that accompanies being routinely regarded as mere bit players in the show that is the history of America.

Yet we strive for the station that God has bestowed upon all men; not to stand beneath or above our white brothers and sisters, but on the same footing, shoulder-to-shoulder, as equals. Sadly, as we demonstrate our humanity and right to claim life, liberty, and the pursuit of happiness as guaranteed by our nation's founding documents, we live in the knowledge that as sure as the sun rises, our selves or any one of our beloveds could become the next murdered and martyred trending topic or rallying cry by day's end.

This most recent spate of hate against Black bodies in white spaces has opened the eyes of many white Americans. But it has taken a deluge of camera phone footage documenting the murders of Black men, women, and children to convince large numbers of white people that America has a chronic anti-Black racism problem. These impromptu documentaries substantiate what Black people experience, witness, and testify to in courts daily, what white minds refuse to imagine possible or believe: Black lives are routinely being snuffed out at the hands of law enforcement officers and garden variety racists. With impunity and paid administrative leave. Now any random bystander can become a bona fide eyewitness to the murder of a Black body and upload it to the social media platform of their choice for all the world to see.

The shockwaves from this shift in the nation's consciousness have been seismic. Americans from coast to coast are re-examining the country's relationship with anti-Black racism and the symbols used to tell America's history. Confederate monuments are coming down—some taken down forcibly by citizens, others quietly removed without fanfare by local and state mandates. NASCAR stunned the public and infuriated a sizable section of its fanbase when it banned the Confederate flag from its events. Corporations have issued full-throated statements of support for Black Lives Matter. Whether future deeds will align with present words remains to be seen, but it's a long overdue and welcome step in the right direction. Even the state of Mississippi, the last to still display the Confederate battle flag, recently voted to remove the stars and bars from its state flag.

Even during the global COVID-19 pandemic, the sheer number of demonstrations and participants who have marched in opposition to the systemic racism and police brutality perpetrated against Black people has been unlike anything seen before in this country. In the streets of Minneapolis, New York, Seattle, Los Angeles, San Francisco, Chicago, and Atlanta, in hundreds of metropolitan areas and thousands of small towns around the United States, people of all ages, all ethnicities, shapes, sizes, and vocations have marched in protest. In Philadelphia on June 6, up to 80,000 people marched in solidarity and support of the notion that Black lives are to be valued.

This time is unlike any other in the planet's history. People are taking part in a movement, not a moment. While hundreds of thousands of people have participated in demonstrations, there are many more who want to take part in realizing a more equitable world, for whom demonstrating is not a viable option. And that's okay. Not everyone has to be the tip of the spear. There's plenty more work to be done. Much more.

Our Human Family creates programs and educational tools to help people advocate for racial equality and inclusion. We know there are people who are unsure of where, when, or how to get involved. We saw this as an opportunity to provide them with a handbook of sorts to help prepare them for the work of equality and anti-racism. And *Fieldnotes on Allyship: Achieving Equality Together* was born.

Fieldnotes on Allyship is inspired by scientists' established practice of taking notes on what they observe while out in the field. We extend its function into its design by providing generous side and bottom margins for you to jot down your observations and ruminations.

Fieldnotes on Allyship is an anthology of real-world observations on:

1. the precise nature of racism
2. the forces that maintain systemic racism
3. the preparations necessary to do the work of equality and anti-racism, and
4. actionable ways to facilitate equality in support of Black, Indigenous, and People of Color (BIPOC), right where you are.

CLAY RIVERS

These seventeen chapters were written by authors and writers from the United States and around the world. They include anti-racism activists, authors, artists, a Masters Athlete, college professors, a retired U.S. Navy sailor, political pundits, an attorney, and anthropologists. They're mothers, fathers, daughters, sons, sisters, and brothers—all of various ethnicities. Some names you may already know, others you may not; but by the time you read to the end of this book, their collective stories—written with integrity, empathy, and an occasional sprinkling of humor—will live in your heart and mind.

Our Human Family positions allyship as a longterm, perhaps even lifelong, commitment to the process of learning, growing, and advancement of equality. We believe that allyship is not a performative checklist of steps one completes to obtain a merit badge. Standing up for equality is its own reward. The moniker "ally" is not a self-appointed Napoleonic crown one proclaims to laud dominion over the lives of mere marginalized people. No. Being an ally is an unsolicited honor that is earned through supporting marginalized people in their fight for equality and demonstrating trust that we are the best experts on our lived experiences and needs.

And marginalized people of any ethnicity hold no less expertise because they have not been certified as such by an institution or because they are not fluent in the latest social justice lingo. For example, in my early twenties, as a Black man living in the South, I was all too aware that society lavished unmerited benefits on white people that Black people rarely, if ever, experienced. And now, a few decades later, the term "white privilege" has become common parlance. Who better to understand the experiences of what it is to be Black than someone who wakes up Black in the morning, is Black throughout the day, and is still Black when they shut their eyes at night? Serving as an ally hinges upon actively listening to those stories, and treating those served with respect and care. As you'll discover much later in Section IV, those experiences can be known; but then, the service of an ally isn't a zero-sum game in which total and complete understanding are prerequisites.

Equality and the eradication of racism are complicated subjects that require nuance in their presentation, explanation, and assimilation. No one has all the answers in solving America's problematic relationship with equality and racism, and we at Our Human Family and the authors of *Fieldnotes on Allyship* are not so naive as to assume that we are presenting all of them here. Because of our varied lived experiences, those of our readers, the fluid nature of words, and their subjective interpretation, it's incumbent upon me to at least try to start us all on the same page. Throughout this book the terms Black, People of Color, and the acronym BIPOC are used extensively, *but not interchangeably*. Volumes have been written about the interpretation of these expressions and are as varied as there are opinions about who should be named as the greatest basketball player of all time. What follows are my most basic working definitions of those terms given within the context of me living as a Black man, in the southern United States, in the year 2020.

As you may have guessed, *Fieldnotes on Allyship* is a direct response to the racism enacted against Black people in the United States. This is not at the patent exclusion or denial of enslaved Black or any other people outside the United States, it simply means *this is our first and foremost point of discussion.*

· · ·

BLACK As discussed within these pages refers primarily to the descendants of the various cultures of Africa who were brought to the British colonies, enslaved, and scattered across the United States. Yes, this includes people who have one parent who is a descendant of those enslaved people and another parent of different ethnicity. "Black" within these pages is not a pejorative, a put-down, or some linguistic sleight of hand. We use it unapologetically and with intentionality to recognize the inherent humanity, dignity, culture, and significance of people of the African diaspora.

BROWN The term as we use it, refers to people of Latin and Hispanic ethnicity, as well as but not limited to non-white people of Middle Eastern countries.

PEOPLE OF COLOR (POC) Now here's where things get tricky. Given Our Human Family's life-affirming regard for all people, we use this phrase to encompass Black and other non-white people around the world, including Asia, and Indigenous Australians, while collectively respecting their individual struggles for equality, dignity, and autonomy. We do not use it to diminish, erase, or ignore their endeavors. And we note that the designation can be problematic. There is a tendency for people to use People of Color interchangeably when Black is far more honest and accurate. For example, if you consider "people of color" within the setting of segregation in the 1960s, the term is limiting and restrictive in that segregation efforts were inordinately directed at Black people.

BLACK, INDIGENOUS, AND PEOPLE OF COLOR (BIPOC) This phrase, used mostly in reference to the United States, emphasizes the oppression experienced by Black and Indigenous people, including Asian, Hispanic, Latin, and Pacific Islanders, but *not* at the exclusion of other ethnicities not mentioned here who may reside in North America. This term is not meant to create a hierarchy of trauma or distress. All oppression is detrimental to the oppressed.

WHITE People characterized by light pigmentation of their skin. Currently, the dominant culture in America rooted in western European traditions. We won't delve into how the notion of "white" came to be here. Fear not; "whiteness" is a topic all unto itself that is addressed in greater detail in Part II.

• • •

I cannot stress this enough: These terms are abbreviations of sorts for the most complicated and intricate creatures on Earth—humans. Just know that our intention is not diminish the dignity of any human being, but to serve a greater good. Defining terms that are infinitely subjective is problematic at best, no matter how we slice it.

As you may have gathered, without the overarching construct of race and racism, there's no need for the labels, bigotry, or racism. That's the world we're hoping to inspire you to create. And we do hope that *Fieldnotes on Allyship* broadens your understanding of your Black brothers and sisters, of the wonderful commonalities we share with you, and the gloriously radiant ways we are different. Because once you see someone as human, you can never unsee their humanity.

We invite you to join us on our journey to achieve equality for all members of our human family.

Love one another.

Clay Rivers
PRESIDENT, OUR HUMAN FAMILY

FOREWORD

Clay Rivers is an author, award-winning art director, accidental activist, president of the nonprofit organization Our
Human Family, Inc. and founder and editorial director of
the Medium publication of the same name. Both the nonprofit and the publication reflect one of his core beliefs:
People change when they *want* to change, when they *know*
change is possible, and when they know *how* to change.

PREFACE

SHERRY KAPPEL

PANDEMICS ASIDE, 2020 HAS been a strange new world. Certainly for many white people, it's been disconcerting to move from blissful unawareness, or perhaps a vague sense that Black people were exaggerating their woes, to an overwhelming preponderance of proof that racism is not only real but is in fact common and often deadly. Meanwhile, Black people are receiving levels of support they haven't seen since the Civil Rights Era—if ever. But can they trust us white folks? How long will our support last? How far are we willing to go to help, especially when it conflicts with our own interests?

A frequently used term for a supportive person of any demographic who's seen the light and wishes to help others pursue justice and equality is "ally"; hence this book's title. What does it actually mean, though? What must one know to be an ally? What are the expectations? What work is required? Is this truly our fight?

The term "ally" is somewhat loaded, in part because of all those questions. People of Color, even those who've lived relatively unscathed, understand racism at the deepest level: what it means, what it looks like, how their lives can change in an instant. Most white people, however, still have much to learn, and not just about racism but also about themselves. Our hearts may be in the right place, but how easy is it to confront Uncle Joe, especially at a family gathering? We want to step into heated situations, but what if that angry antagonist pulls a knife? And reparations are a financial and logistical nightmare . . . how could we possibly support those? So, even with the best intentions, we find ourselves falling down on the job—while Black and Brown people shake their heads in frustration, questioning the point of allies.

The safety pin debacle several years ago is a good example. For those who might not remember, it was suggested that would-be allies wear a safety pin in an obvious place so that a Person of Color would know where they could turn for assistance or even defense. It sounded like a good idea to many Liberals. The reality, though, is that most pin-wearers hadn't really thought it through very well. In fact, for many it had more to do with showing off their moral correctness than helping anyone at all. *Black heads shaking.*

Other issues with being an "ally" include that it's not just something you can label yourself; like beauty, it must be in the eye of the beholder. If People of Color don't consider you an ally, you most assuredly are not. And beyond that, people and situations are constantly changing and evolving. Racism itself evolves. You cannot do a good deed, hang the "ally medal" around your neck, and settle back. It's something you must work on continuously. So instead of concerning ourselves with a label, we should just get to work.

Please understand, no one expects the average ally to know every sordid detail of Black history in America and every nuance of racism, or carry a machete and come out swinging at the hint of a microaggression. We each bring different skills to the table, and not everyone—regardless of color—is meant to lead a protest. Some are better writers than speakers. But to qualify as an ally, it is not enough to have a big heart and yet do nothing. As Martin Luther King Jr. noted in his "Letter from Birmingham Jail," "Shallow understanding from people of goodwill is more frustrating than absolute misunderstanding from people of ill will. Lukewarm acceptance is much more bewildering than outright rejection." So the question I'd ask you to consider as you read this book and self-define going forward is: *How committed are you to true equality?*

SHERRY KAPPEL

• • •

Fieldnotes on Allyship was written to help you on your journey as an ally. It isn't meant to provide all the answers, but rather the foundation for understanding and finding your path. Some of the authors are writers, while others are simply passionate about achieving the elusive American ideals we grew up hearing about, of all people being created equal in this land of opportunity. Some of the authors are Black, others Brown or white; some are men, some women; they hail from several continents. Because, regardless of our backgrounds and experiences, everyone here believes as Maya Angelou wrote in her poem "Human Family," "We are more alike, my friends, than unalike."

Finally, I have to say how honored I am to participate in this book. Certainly there are many great authors and essays in here, and information that can help you learn and grow. However, I'm especially grateful as a white woman—all too often seen as the "enemy" or a questionable ally—to serve as an editor. When Black and Brown authors have been hurt repeatedly by people who look much like me, and *still* place their words—essentially, their hearts—in my hands, it requires enormous trust that I will honor their writing and lived experience. I hope I have and will continue to earn it.

Sherry Kappel
OUR HUMAN FAMILY, SPECIAL PROJECTS EDITOR

Sherry Kappel is a poet, essayist, and fiction writer with an MFA from the University of Pittsburgh. She looks for the best in humanity and is driven by empathy in her writing and in life. Her work is on Medium, where she also edits *Snapshots, the Haiku Hub,* and special projects for *Our Human Family.* Sherry lives in North Carolina with her husband, daughters, and critters.

INTRODUCTION

UNDOING RACISM: WHY DEFINITIONS MATTER

TIM WISE

Though it may sound cliché, it is increasingly apparent that America stands at a crossroads. As COVID-19 continues to devastate the nation, and with Black and Latinx folks two to three times more likely than whites to perish from the illness, we are witnessing mass death in real time. This, combined with the racial justice uprising in response to the police killing of George Floyd, has the United States poised on the brink of something momentous, or so it seems. What that might be, and in which direction the nation may turn, is yet to be determined.

But whatever the decision, it will, as it always does, involve a choice between racial oppression and multiracial democracy. Those are the only two destinations on this road we travel. They have always been the only two places on the national map.

To this point, we have spent far more of our time in the former than in the latter. Indeed, we have only briefly attempted to even locate the second of these before hurrying back to the first, apparently more comfortable in the familiar environs of inequality. Well, at least some of us are. And sadly, these have been the ones with the keys, unwilling to ask for directions to the other locale, not wanting to go there anyway, and mightily upset by others in the car insisting the driver should pull over and let someone else navigate for a while.

One hopes this is changing, and perhaps it is. A new generation is rising up, demanding that the nation fulfill its promises, much as those before them demanded the same. In the past few months, millions have poured into the streets in cities and towns across America, insisting that Black lives matter, and that until the nation ratifies this truth in public policy, the justice system, and other institutions of daily life, none of us are free.

And yet, even as we fight to end racism in the hearts, minds, and institutions of the country, one thing could greatly complicate our attempts to accomplish that. Namely, a clear-headed understanding of what it is we're fighting in the first place.

While one might assume we all know the enemy by now—we all know what racism is and how it functions, so that all we need to decide at this point is the proper antidote—I can assure you this is far from true. Get ten random people together in a room and ask them to define racism, and you will get at least a half-dozen different answers, if not one for every person so gathered. As you might imagine, if we can't agree on what we're fighting, defeating it will prove difficult.

Even turning to a dictionary fails to suffice, since dictionary definitions rely more on common agreement than some objective description of reality. And when it comes to the term "racism," both of the dominant definitions raise as many questions as they answer.

According to *Merriam-Webster*, the principal definition of racism is "a belief that race is the primary determinant of human traits and capacities and that racial differences produce an inherent superiority of a particular race." Meanwhile, according to the *New Oxford American Dictionary*, racism is "the belief that all members of each race possess characteristics or abilities specific to that race, especially so as to distinguish it as inferior or superior to another race or races."

But neither of these two renderings seems adequate. For instance, if one rejects the idea that race is the primary determinant of human traits but still believes it to be a significant determiner of them, can that no longer be viewed as racism? If one rejects the idea that one group is inherently superior or inferior (as in, biologically so) but believes that groups have developed broad-based cultural attributes that render them such, should we not consider that person guilty of racism?

Are Black people somehow less at risk of discrimination if millions of people think they are defective because of culturally derived pathologies instead of genetic ones? If I believe Jews are bad people because they have developed a culture of greed and dishonesty, as opposed to what Hitler thought—that Jews were a distinct race of evildoers, driven biologically to destroy Aryan civilization—am I any less an anti-Semite? Of course not. So too, requiring racial prejudice to be rooted in biological assumptions before it can be called racism seems absurd.

Regarding the second definition, must one believe that all members of a certain race possess characteristics that render them superior or inferior before they qualify as racist? If I allow a few exceptions to a generally dysfunctional rule—say, a few Black people with super-high IQs, even as I insist most Black folks are less intelligent than whites—am I no longer guilty of racism? Surely not.

And so we cannot rely on dictionaries. Far too many beliefs that have injured people based on racial category would fly beneath the radar provided by these definitions. No less a bigot than David Duke, former Klan leader and lifelong white supremacist, would fail to qualify as racist under this interpretation. Even Duke has publicly allowed that some Black people are smarter than some white people. He also admits there are "some good Jews," but given his praise for Adolf Hitler and insistence that the Holocaust didn't happen, I'm guessing no one would take that to mean that he isn't an anti-Semite.

To my way of thinking, racism is best understood as two things: an ideology and a system—and this seems true as a simple matter of grammar. After all, when we see words ending with i-s-m, we typically can intuit something about them.

On the one hand, they are ideologies. In this case, the doctrine is one that says certain people, because of their racial category, are in some meaningful way generally better or worse than certain other people from different racial groups. But so too, "isms" are systems—think capitalism, socialism, communism, fascism, authoritarianism, and so on. All are ideologies, as with racism, but they are not merely that. They are not solely ways of thinking about the world and people in it; they are also ways of organizing that world so as to treat those persons quite differently.

At this more concrete level, racism is a system of TIM WISE inequality, where the disparities are reflected in the life chances of (and outcomes obtained by) people in different racial categories. Like all systems, racism is held together by policies, practices, and procedures—some formal and others informal—that create and perpetuate those inequalities. While these policies, practices, and procedures were often crafted by persons in thrall to the ideology of racism, these instruments of inequality can be wielded by those who are not, but who fail to question their normativity or recognize the harm they do.

Some of the policies, practices, and procedures of systemic and institutional racism would have been obvious and deliberate: enslavement, segregation, and redlining of Black neighborhoods by banks, as just a few examples. But others might well have non-racial reasons for their existence, and yet have a foreseeable racially-disparate impact, rendering them worthy of the designation as examples of institutional racism.

To wit, reliance on standardized tests, even in schools with unstandardized resources, unstandardized curricula, and students from profoundly unequal backgrounds. Or a "war on drugs" adopted by law enforcement in the name of crime control, but which has disproportionately targeted Black and Brown bodies, even as white folks possess, use, and deal drugs at comparable rates to people of color. Or relying on the so-called old boys network for hiring decisions, which tends to favor white men, while locking folks of Color out of job opportunities, even without the presence of overt racism.

Even making hiring decisions based on accumulated on-paper credentials can amount to institutional racism if those credentials are not evaluated in their proper context. For white job applicants to look better on paper doesn't necessarily mean they are more qualified. It may indicate they simply had more access to prior opportunities than their counterparts of Color. And if I have a five-lap head start on you in an eight-lap race, I'm supposed to hit the tape first. But when I do, one shouldn't presume I was the faster runner. Indeed, if at the end of the race, I'm only three laps ahead, you were.

So unless employers are thinking critically about the so-called merit indicia they use to make hiring decisions, they could inadvertently perpetuate racial disparity even absent deliberate intent. To the extent the accumulation of credentials is tied to the opportunity structure, handing out the next round of goodies (like jobs, contracts, or college slots) based on such credentials reinforces racism at the systemic level.

Differentiating between the ideology of racism and its systemic manifestations is essential for another reason, too. It allows us to distinguish between racism as a generic notion of group-based superiority or inferiority, and racism as a specific, sedimented structure of unequal opportunity. It enables us to differentiate between racism, the theory, and white supremacy, the practice.

For years people have asked me, for instance, why I focus my attention on white racism while ignoring racism on the part of Black people and other folks of Color. Do I think only white people can be racist? While there is a pat answer typically offered by anti-racist theorists in response to this question—that Black and Brown folks cannot be racist because racism is a systemic reality requiring power to effectuate— my take on it is different. I am more than willing to accept that at the level of ideology, which "isms" are, by definition, anyone can be guilty of racism. But at the systemic level, which is where the rubber meets the road, so to speak, white racism and supremacy is the only actualized form of racism, at least in the U.S. and the larger western world.

So Black people can believe themselves superior and whites inferior and can think all kinds of hateful things about white people. And yes, I am willing to call that racism of a sort. But truthfully, what will such a person be able to do, concretely, with that hatred or set of beliefs? Can they prevent me from obtaining a home or a job because of it? Will I be racially profiled by police based on it? Doubtful.

I suppose they might physically attack me if sufficiently imbued with such anti-white bias. But if the only way you can hurt me is to do something that will put you in the crosshairs of the legal system, you do not have the power. I do. Power is being able to hurt people legally, with the stroke of a pen when it comes to government budgets,

TIM WISE

zoning laws, voting requirements, access to health insurance, and placement in advanced as opposed to remedial school classes. You can stand on the street corner and scream about white people being Satanic devils all day long. I'll see your street theatre and raise you a stop-and-frisk. See the difference?

Think of it like this. When your car is sitting on empty in your driveway, no gas in the tank, the combustion engine under the hood is still an engine. But unless you provide it with a fuel source, it will remain sitting there, inert. Ideological racism is like the engine. Institutional power is the fuel source. If it makes you feel better to say that Black people can be guilty of the first of these, have at it. But good luck demonstrating their ability to drive that shit around town.

And so, when we speak of racism, let us define our terms and be as precise as possible. What we have in America is not just racism. It's white supremacy. It's the difference between the generic "cola" you can pick up at the grocery, and "Coke," which we all know is the brand with the leading market share. And in the case of racism, it's more extreme than that, because there isn't even a racial equivalent of Pepsi.

Okay, enough with the metaphors. You get the point. We must clarify our concepts, broaden our understanding of how racism operates, and acknowledge the enterprise's fundamentally white nature if we are ever to undo its presence in our lives and society.

So now, having clarified the adversary, there is only one thing left for us to do: namely, go forth, and take apart the damned engine.

Tim Wise is among the most prominent anti-racist writers and educators in the United States. He is the author of eight books, including his forthcoming, *Dispatches from the Race War* (December 2020, City Lights). Other books include *Dear White America: Letter to a New Minority* and his highly acclaimed memoir, *White Like Me: Reflections on Race from a Privileged Son.*

PART I

RACISM

WHAT THEY DON'T TEACH IN HISTORY CLASS 1

MICHAEL GREINER, PH.D., J.D.

To MANY, HISTORY IS boring. Most of us remember history class as learning again and again about those white guys from Europe who "explored" America. Never mind that they were actually a bunch of incompetent boobs who thought they had made it to India. Or that they never would have succeeded in their conquests if they didn't bring with them vicious germs. Or that they destroyed societies that were, in many ways, more advanced than those in Europe. Their behavior on behalf of Christianity seemed so unlike what Jesus would do.

And what about the women, or People of Color? Unfortunately for most, history class was monochromatic. No wonder most people hate history.

On the other hand, I was a history major. I love history because it is the story of who we are and how we came to be where we are. In my view, anybody who loved hearing stories from their grandparents about their family lore should love history. Good history is just an expansion upon that story-telling, conveying the story of our American family, and our human family.

Since I recognize the limitations in our history curriculum, I have struggled to find a more inclusive version. At times I have succeeded, at other times not. But finding an inclusive history takes real effort. Most people have neither the time nor the inclination to engage in such an effort. As a result, it is not surprising that to some, over-simplifying the study of history to merely the display of statues is appealing.

Nowadays, we are engaged in a national discussion over what American history is. Is it really just represented by monuments, or is it something else entirely? In effect, do monuments accurately represent "our" history?

The debate over monuments is perhaps more telling than many would like to recognize. I remember when I was in college in the 1980s, my grandmother chafing at the idea of somebody majoring in African American Studies or Women's Studies. "They should just major in history," she would argue. But the word "history" itself reveals its bias: it is an amalgam of "his story." What about the *hers*?

Putting up a monument takes money and access to other resources. As a result, most people don't put up monuments. Oftentimes, government will put up a monument. In those cases, then, putting up a monument requires political power. What this fact reveals to us is that the existence of a monument in and of itself is a reflection of the views of people with money and power. Very rarely will people without money or power be represented in a monument.

Furthermore, as any economist will tell you, financial resources are limited. You can choose to spend your money and political capital on a monument, or you can spend it on food, a house, an education, luxury goods, you name it. The point is that building a monument takes commitment. You need a reason to build it. No monument was ever built, especially given their high cost, *just because.*

MICHAEL GREINER, PH.D., J.D.

OF MONUMENTS AND MESSAGING

So why are people willing to spend their hard-earned money and political power on monuments? They want to tell a story. More importantly, they want to make a point. Consider the monuments dedicated to Confederate officers. Most of these monuments were not constructed right after the war. Most were instead erected by The United Daughters of the Confederacy in the 1890s with the aim of glorifying the Confederacy as a "lost cause." This myth would whitewash the history of the South, ignoring the basis of its rebellion—slavery—and instead painting a heroic picture.

Consider the following: a brief review of *Wikipedia* reveals that there are far more monuments to Confederate

General Robert E. Lee, a former U.S. Army officer who committed treason against the country he swore an oath to, than there are to Union General Ulysses S. Grant. Grant, of course, is likely more responsible than any person other than Abraham Lincoln for saving the Union. He was the Union general who defeated the Confederacy, and later as president, he defeated the earliest iteration of the Ku Klux Klan. However, there are more memorials to the Confederacy's president, Jefferson Davis, and Confederate officer Thomas "Stonewall" Jackson, than there are to Grant. How could this be? The reason is that the Confederate apologists wanted to spread their myth far and wide, while most Northerners simply wanted to put the Civil War behind us.

But it is not just monuments that represent a point of view. Especially in the era before the internet, it was hard to distribute information. Printing and distribution of books, magazines, and pamphlets was prohibitively expensive. As a result, publishers acted as gatekeepers to the public discourse. Until relatively recently, those gatekeepers were almost exclusively wealthy white men. Even if they held a liberal, open-minded point of view, their decisions would inevitably be colored by their own experience. If you have never personally experienced violent oppression, it is unlikely that you will consider it a worthwhile subject for a book.

Similarly, the practice of history takes time and commitment. Few have the training or the time to do the in-depth research required for historical analysis. As a result, that group too was primarily wealthy, white, and male, resulting in choices of subjects to research, books to write, and classes to teach that reflected their own background.

The quote attributed to Winston Churchill that "History is written by the victors" reflects that fact. Consider how white Americans painted the First Nations as the aggressors through much of history. As a child, I remember playing "cowboys and Indians." You can guess who the good guys were. We remember Custer's annihilation at Little Big Horn, but how many examples of the genocide of Native Americans are most people familiar with? Thinking of the First Nations as the aggressors doesn't even make sense. After all, white people were taking the land they were already on. And yet, until recently, the white majority has excused its inexcusable behavior of the past by whitewashing this history.

MICHAEL GREINER, PH.D., J.D.

Obviously, a similar whitewashing has occurred regarding white Americans' shameful treatment of Black people for centuries. There are those who equate Black people being brought across the ocean in shackles to be enslaved, with the challenges faced by immigrant groups who came here voluntarily. There are those who even call the 400 years of slavery a "choice" by those enslaved. And, there are those who excuse the enslavement of Africans because the victims were generally captured by other Black people.

Nevertheless, most Americans know that the slavery existed, and that it was brutal. What most Americans likely do not know about is how little life improved for most Black people after the Civil War. In the post-bellum South, after the brief promise of Reconstruction came to an end, the same people who had dominated Southern society prior to the war once again attained dominance

7

in Southern society after the war. In many places, however, they achieved this dominance despite the fact that they might have been in the minority given the numbers of liberated Black people. How did they gain this power given the fact that the numbers were not on their side, and the United States was purportedly a democracy?

STATE-SANCTIONED TERRORISM

The goal of the white men who had held the power in the South prior to the Civil War was to regain their privilege, even though the war and subsequent constitutional amendments had supposedly torn down the institutions of the antebellum South. These old institutions had granted them power over People of Color through slavery. So they worked to recreate the essence of slavery through Jim Crow laws even though the new legal regime purported to eliminate it.

The pre-war white elite accomplished this goal through a number of strategies. First and foremost was terror. A visit to the National Memorial for Peace and Justice in Montgomery, Alabama, otherwise known as the National Lynching Memorial, will shake any sentient human being to their core: the very idea that in this supposed nation of laws, more than 4,000 documented lynchings of African Americans took place between 1877 and 1950. In virtually all cases, those who committed these crimes went unpunished. But that fact misses the point. The lynchings, mostly concentrated in the twelve Southern states that made up the slavery block prior to the Civil War, were state-sanctioned terrorism, designed to keep Black people from asserting their constitutional rights.

Consider the massacre in Elaine, Arkansas in 1919. Black soldiers, who had served with distinction in World War I, returned home to find a society where Black sharecroppers were treated similarly to enslaved people prior to the Civil War. Having been feted for their bravery by our French allies, these former soldiers decided to do something about their treatment back home and started organizing a union. This Union would demand some political and economic rights for Black people in this former Confederate slave state.

This peaceful meeting was such a threat to the white establishment of the area that the local sheriff led an attack on the Black community. Troops from the local U.S. Army base used automatic weapons that had recently been wielded by soldiers in Europe to kill dozens. White mobs roamed freely attacking Black Americans. As many as 800 Black people were killed in the massacre.

MICHAEL GREINER, PH.D., J.D.

The response? Not a single white person was arrested. Instead, the sheriff arrested 285 Black people, ultimately resulting in charges being brought against 122 of them. Twelve of those were sentenced to death in trials that lasted only minutes.

Eventually the Supreme Court would invalidate the conviction of those twelve, holding that since they were tortured with electrical shocks on their genitals, refused access to counsel, and tried by jury with a mob gathered outside the courthouse, these twelve Black men had been denied due process. This ruling was small comfort, however. Although none of them would be put to death as a result of these charges, most served years in prison.

This was just one such massacre. Dozens of massacres occurred throughout the South, many as bad or worse than the Elaine attack. Given the tacit approval such violence earned from the state by supporting the aggressors and failing to prosecute them, these massacres were nothing short of state-sanctioned terrorism, aimed at terrorizing People of Color. The message was clear: when Black people seek fair treatment, they risk their lives and the lives of those they care about.

DENIAL OF ECONOMIC OPPORTUNITY

The second approach taken by the white communities was the denial of economic opportunity. Most people are well aware of the lunch counters reserved for white people only. Such discrimination was allowed, so goes the theory, because it was engaged in by private citizens. In other words, if there is no government action involved, it is okay for them to discriminate. We see shadows of this judicial philosophy today in such cases as the *Masterpiece Cakeshop v. Colorado* decision, which allowed private bakers to discriminate against gay people.

But separate lunch counters were only the beginning. We know about transportation, with the separate seating in buses and separate cars in trains. But do we know that in Alabama, it was illegal for a Black person and a white person to play dominoes or checkers together, or that in Georgia people of different races couldn't play baseball within two blocks of each other, or that Oklahoma required the separation of races when fishing or boating, or that Arkansas segregated its horse-racing tracks? In effect, Black people were not allowed free access to the economy.

In response, some Black people started their own businesses. But when these became too successful, that too was a threat to the white establishment. Only recently have many of us become aware of the massacre in Tulsa, Oklahoma in 1921 in which white residents burned the Greenwood District, a successful Black community popularly known as Black Wall Street, to the ground. Many of the attackers had been deputized by the sheriff and were given weapons by city officials as a result. Over 300 Black residents were killed, 800 more were injured, and over 5,000 people were left homeless. Of course, no white people were convicted for this crime.

MICHAEL GREINER, PH.D., J.D.

Thus, a message was sent: don't try to participate in our economy, and don't try to build your own economy in response.

LEGAL ATTACKS

The final prong of the effort to oppress Black people came in the form of legal attacks. After the Civil War, three amendments had been added to the Constitution. The Thirteenth Amendment banned slavery. The Fourteenth Amendment guaranteed all Americans due process of law, and clarified that anyone born on U.S. territory, no matter what the color of their skin, is entitled to all the rights of citizenship. Finally, the Fifteenth Amendment guaranteed Black men the right to vote.

In response, the powers-that-be launched a full-fledged assault upon these newly granted rights, especially the right to vote, since Southern Black voters had sufficient numbers to dramatically affect state policy. In response,

Southern states began requiring voters to pay a poll tax to vote, or to pass a literacy test. Although these requirements often placed a heavier burden upon Black people, who were denied educational and economic opportunities, because the law did not specifically disenfranchise Black people, it was held to not violate equal protection. In other words, if a law is applied to everyone, even if it has a greater impact upon Black people, it passes constitutional muster. As recently as 1959, the Supreme Court reaffirmed this view in *Lassiter v. Northampton County Board of Elections*.

But we do not need to go back that far, nor do we need to go to the former slave states, to see examples of legalized discrimination. It was under President Woodrow Wilson in the 1910s that the federal government was fully segregated. In the 1930s, as part of the New Deal's effort to make more housing available, laws mandated the segregation of our housing stock. And the purported "war on drugs" initiated in the 1970s by Richard Nixon and still ongoing today has become a means to harass and imprison America's Black men. As recently as 2011, an astounding 685,724 people, almost all of them young Black and Latino men, were stopped by police in New York without basis as part of its "stop and frisk" policy. That policy, by the way, was allowable under a 1968 Supreme Court decision, *Terry v. Ohio*.

THE TROUBLING REGULARITY OF DISCRIMINATION

For years, though, white liberals such as myself were able to convince ourselves that the complaints of Black people over discrimination were overstated. After all, we had never seen police behave in the way Black people described. It was only in 1991 when George Holliday videotaped from his back porch police attacking Rodney King that most of us saw such violence firsthand. And even then, it seemed as if this behavior was the exception rather than the rule. When the police officers were acquitted for their actions, we were outraged. After all, such exceptional behavior needed to be purged from our police forces, right?

We had no idea how widespread this behavior was. What really changed everything was the cell phone. Now, just about everyone carries in their pocket a high-quality video recorder. The result has been dozens of Rodney King videos, each more egregious than the other. No longer can liberal white people believe that such behavior by police is exceptional. No longer can we claim Black people are overstating the violence they experience at the hands of the police. No longer can moral people look the other way. Now, the evidence is plain for everyone to see.

MICHAEL GREINER, PH.D., J.D.

The response has been dramatic. For the first time in history, Gallup polls find that most people—even most white Americans—support the people protesting police actions. This is a significant change. Today an overwhelming number of Americans look up to Dr. Martin Luther King Jr., but at the time, he and his protests were viewed negatively by a wide margin. Hopefully, this new change in perspective might finally mean that we can address the stain of racism that continues to afflict our nation— whether that's considering the needs of others when voting, standing up for People of Color in conversations, donating to Black Lives Matter, or demanding that your libraries and local schools provide more accurate history books. The question is, what will each of us do to see these changes through, ensuring that racial parity is finally achieved and American history going forward reflects the ideals we have always claimed to hold: with liberty, and justice for all.

Michael Greiner, Ph.D., J.D. combines practical experience with scholarship. As a political activist, he managed campaigns across the country, worked on Capitol Hill, and served as Deputy Mayor of Warren, Michigan's third largest city. As an attorney, he practiced Bankruptcy law, founding his own firm that helped thousands of families and businesses restructure their debts. As a scholar, his research has been published in top journals including *The Harvard Business Review, The Journal of Business Strategy,* and *The Journal of Business Research.*

THE BLIGHT OF SYSTEMIC RACISM 2

LECIA MICHELLE

C HANGE IS COMING. AMERICANS take to the street protesting the murders of Black people by police. Every
day more are joining the fight. In response to the movement, corporations release statements supporting Black
lives; cities remove Confederate statues; and Aunt Jemima
disappears from a syrup bottle and pancake mix box.

*No statement, rebranded syrup bottle, or missing statue
will end systemic racism.*

In July 2020, Ijeoma Oluo, author of *So You Want to
Talk About Race*, discussed systemic racism with NPR's
Noel King. She explains it this way:

"What's actually been impacting our lives are systems that rely on subtle and not so subtle biases against People of Color to disempower us and put us at risk. And so we've been fighting for job opportunities, for safety from violence, for equal education, for freedom from medical racism. And that is upheld not by how you love or don't love People of Color but by how you participate with our systems."

Systemic racism affects every aspect of Black and Brown lives. Words and performative responses won't change that. No new name will solve it. That's because systemic racism permeates every educational entity, corporation, financial institution, and community. Simply put, it's everywhere. The fight must be taken to its strongholds. We do need people to protest, and while it's fine to remove those symbols of oppression, we must do more. That means looking at our educational systems, financial institutions, workplace environments, and healthcare systems.

Eradicating systemic racism means that white people don't benefit from their skin color, and Black and Brown people aren't punished for theirs. That means every unfair advantage and disadvantage based on race disappears. It means white people no longer move to the head of the line simply for being white. It means every benefit that makes their lives easier for being white people no longer exists. It means they don't expect to automatically be considered first for opportunities in which they aren't a fair recipient. This means changing their mindset that they have the right to this easier life that ensures they navigate a smoother path and are guaranteed their children follow that same path. It means not using the police as a tool to oppress Black and Brown people.

EARLY EXPOSURE

Some school systems seek to end partnerships with local police departments. Why is this important? Because teachers are more likely to call the police on Black and Brown students they deem to be disciplinary problems. These encounters can start with children as young as five years old. A video of six-year-old Kaia Rolle being handcuffed and led off by a policeman was widely circulated over the internet. She can be heard sobbing as she is taken out of school and put into a police car. Her crime? Throwing a tantrum, a common occurrence in children but criminal when that child is Black—even at six! Kaia will remember that day for the rest of her life. Never mind that the policeman was fired. He's not scarred for life. The 2020 *EdSource* article "Should police officers be in schools? California educators rethink school safety" explains how the mere presence of police officers in schools can cause stress for Black and Brown students. Many of their parents have already given them "the talk." This talk is a rite of passage for most of them. Their parents explain how to survive an encounter with the police—although there are no guarantees, even after this talk, that they will survive. In the article, opponents of police presence in schools further explain: "For those students, interactions with school police are often their introduction to the criminal justice system and the beginning of what has been dubbed the "school-to-prison pipeline."

LECIA
MICHELLE

19

Black and Brown students aren't safe if that school system sees them as criminals instead of students. One would hope teachers are less racist because they choose to work with Black and Brown children. Sadly, this is untrue. If they're willing to call 911 when a child is acting out, they're willing to participate in a white supremacist hierarchy that puts Black and Brown children at the mercy of teachers, administrators, and security personnel. School becomes just another place where they can be abused, neglected and marginalized.

White parents send their children to school believing they will be safe. Unlike Black and Brown parents, they don't think about the peril their kids could face every day when they walk through those school doors. Their children don't face adults who see them as problems to be handled instead of kids to be nurtured and educated. Systemic racism affects Black and Brown people from an early age. It continues throughout their entire lives. It never subsides. It never lets up. It follows them like an ominous shadow preventing them from experiencing the autonomy and equality white people take for granted.

Education can and should help fight systemic racism. Those formative years are key when preparing children for college. Consider the difficulty of learning in an environment where students feel unsafe simply because of the color of their skin. These schools are terrorizing students and obviously not preparing them to successfully complete high school. For too many, college seems unattainable. Education isn't a cure-all for the racism they will face their entire lives, but it gives those students the opportunity to fill those roles that can bring about real change. Black and

Brown students can attend college or trade school. They can become CEOs, business owners, school administrators, bank presidents, and so many other influential positions where systemic racism currently allows people to put into place barriers for others to attain the American dream.

LIBRARIES TRY TO BRIDGE THE GAP

Many people take internet access for granted. However, struggling families—already worried about keeping their lights on and food in their bellies—can't afford Internet access. That means, when their children have homework that requires Internet access, they depend on schools and public libraries. However, even libraries fall prey to systemic racism.

Libraries are an important part of any neighborhood. The quality of libraries depends on funding. Like public schools, libraries in wealthier (usually white) communities have more computers, better collections, and plenty of funding to provide free educational programming to supplement traditional education. Communities often depend on libraries to provide quality educational support and strong partnerships with local schools. While these partnerships are common, schools and libraries in poorer communities have less money to spend and thus are limited in the programming and educational resources they can provide for their students. They are historically underfunded and do the best they can with the funds they receive. When those funds are dependent on struggling cities with budgets already stretched thin, libraries can only provide a band-aid to the problem of a substandard education.

LECIA
MICHELLE

21

As a librarian working on the front lines serving the public, I've seen firsthand how libraries struggle to support the community. During lean budget years, the library is one of the first departments to face budget cuts. This means less programming and books. It means no extra staff to help with the daily duties that keep a library running smoothly. It means fewer opportunities to bridge the digital divide because less money also means fewer computers, fewer classes on technology use, and fewer staff who can assist with technical support. Technology assistance is one of the main reasons people visit the library. They come to use a library computer, bring their own computer, or ask questions about an electronic device. We are the only free resource they have for this service. Without it, that community will fall even further behind with technology.

HOME OWNERSHIP

Buying a home is an American dream for people of all colors, and a way to build financial equity. People plan. They save. They contact a realtor and begin the process. Black and Brown people can't imagine that there are some realtors who won't show homes in communities whose residents wouldn't want them moving in. Realtors won't tell them this, so prospective buyers would never know unless they specifically requested to see a particular home. It's how white communities attempt to stay white. It's how white people keep "others" out of their neighborhoods. Post-slavery, there were no laws against forcing non-white people into certain communities and keeping them out of others. While it's no longer legal, it's not uncommon to find neighborhoods where Black and Brown people aren't welcome. Realtors know of these places, and some are even complicit in discriminating against non-white people hoping to buy a home there.

Looking for a new home is the easy part, though. Financing that home can be challenging. Historically, financial institutions have made it harder for Black and Brown people to acquire loans. In too many cases, either they're denied a loan outright or approved for a loan at a much higher interest rate, making them a higher risk of defaulting on that loan. Additionally, lack of generational wealth makes it even harder for them to purchase a home. As white people receive more favorable loan terms and many turn to family for help with down payments, non-white people struggle to scrape together a down payment. They also pay private mortgage insurance (PMI) because they don't have the required twenty-percent down payment to avoid this additional fee.

THE EFFECTS OF PREDATORY LENDING

Lenders targeted Black and Brown people for predatory loans during the housing boom of 2006. According to the 2013 *Bloomberg* article "The Dramatic Racial Bias of Subprime Lending During the Housing Boom," "In 2006, at the height of the boom, Black and Hispanic families making more than $200,000 a year were more likely on average to be given a subprime loan than a white family making less than $30,000 a year." The article explains the perfect storm. Lenders who had previously overlooked

LECIA
MICHELLE

Black and Brown families seeking home loans soon saw them as a means to staggering wealth. These high-risk loans had devastating effects on families.

Subprime loans, later called predatory loans, were supposed to help people with less than ideal credit purchase a home. They have high interest rates that increase over time. As interest rates rise, so does the monthly payment. As families struggle to afford these higher mortgage payments, their loan balances increase, making it difficult to build equity in their homes.

A 2016 article in *The Atlantic* entitled "Why Blacks and Hispanics Have Such Expensive Mortgages" discusses the consequences of these high-interest, high-risk loans. Families are unable to pass on wealth to their children to help them pay for college or purchase their own homes. The article explains that, while past practices (such as redlining—per *Brittanica.com*, a practice mortgage lenders use to restrict financial services, deny loans, and unfairly penalize borrowers in African American and mixed communities) are partly to blame for why Black and Brown families lag far behind white families in regards to homeownership, the fact that these groups are still regularly given these riskier loans is also a problem.

The 2016 study "What Drives Racial and Ethnic Differences in High Cost Mortgages? The Role of High Risk Lenders" concluded that race and ethnicity did determine whether a loan applicant was directed toward a high-risk loan product. The *Bloomberg* article further explained, "[E]ven after controlling for general risk considerations, such as credit score, loan-to-value ratio, subordinate liens, and debt-to-income ratios, Hispanic Americans are seventy-eight percent more likely to be given a high-cost mortgage, and Black Americans are 105 percent more likely."

The Atlantic article also discusses how lenders aggressively pursued these communities, knowing they were more vulnerable to accepting less than ideal loan terms. As stated in the aforementioned *Bloomberg* article, even with a good financial profile, Black and Brown people were pushed into riskier loans, which oftentimes meant higher or adjustable interest rates. Higher interest rates make it harder for people to pay down principal balances and build equity.

LECIA
MICHELLE

RACISM IN THE WORKPLACE

American workers spend the majority of their waking hours at work. Systemic racism plays a part in the way hiring, promotions, and assignments are handled. White people are accustomed to having their needs met. Whether those needs are having the boss's ear or receiving a coveted promotion, white people don't consider the experiences of their non-white coworkers. Their internal dialogues consist of conversations justifying the decision not to hire a clearly qualified non-white candidate over a less-than-qualified white one. Why? Because white candidates fit better into the "company culture." In other words, they look like the people making the hiring decisions. They maintain the status quo.

Most white people stay silent when they see blatantly discriminatory hiring practices. They will also support the decision to fire a Black or Brown person. They tell themselves that person didn't fit in or they were too opinionated. White people won't admit that they see racism in their workplace. It's easier to stay silent and reap the benefits. They don't consider the lonely existence of seeing so few, if any, people of one's own race or ethnicity. They don't ask. They don't think about it. They don't care.

HEALTHCARE DISPARITIES

Healthcare disparities in Black and Brown communities are another problem. These groups receive a lower standard of care than their white counterparts. Because of this, they are misdiagnosed or undiagnosed. They never know about the ailments that will eventually lead to other complications and oftentimes a premature death. Black mothers are one such group affected by systemic racism in the health care system.

According to the Centers for Disease Control and Prevention (CDC), Black women are three times more likely to die during pregnancy or from child-birth complications than white women. These deaths cross socio-economic lines, so poverty isn't the reason. Tennis star Serena Williams experienced a pulmonary embolism after giving birth to her daughter. She was outspoken about how privileged she was to have a great team of doctors and nurses. She knows her experience could have been much different if she weren't a celebrity.

Most people don't question their healthcare professionals. They do what is recommended and take what is prescribed. While there are great doctors and nurses, there are also ones who provide a less rigorous standard of care for non-white patients. In this case, systemic racism doesn't just oppress people. It kills them.

How many cases have there been of a misdiagnosis where the patient's ailment was treatable but the proper tests weren't run to ensure an accurate diagnosis? Black and Brown people must be vigilant in the doctor's office. The relationship between doctor and patient should be one of mutual respect. A good doctor encourages their patients to ask questions so they're clear on the information they receive. Unfortunately, because their lives can be at risk, Black and Brown patients must advocate for themselves and speak up when something is unclear or doesn't feel right.

WHERE WE GO FROM HERE

Systemic racism invades every aspect of our society. It's become such a commonplace part of many institutions and communities, that it feels normal to those not experiencing it. Still, everyone must fight it by seeking an education about other cultures and experiences. Although much of this can be accomplished online, get first-hand experiences by attending discussions on racism, visiting museums, and diversifying one's circle of friends. Do not ask Black and Brown people for a free education; it forces them to relive painful life experiences. Just listen and learn.

Parents also must discuss racism with their children. Children are capable of understanding the basics. Visit a local library for books on how to have this discussion or Google ideas on how to begin the conversation. Children know right from wrong. Clearly state that racism is wrong

LECIA
MICHELLE

27

and explain why. Children know when they're angry or sad. Frame the discussion in terms that relate to the emotions people feel when they experience racism. Model the right behavior. Parents should never use racist language, and when they hear such language, call it out. They must let their children know racism is never okay.

Adults in general must take a firm stance against racism. Their families must know they are anti-racist—that they actively fight racism everywhere they see it. Anti-racists won't tolerate hatred in their presence. They embrace being uncomfortable. Fighting racism—especially systemic racism—means speaking up in the workplace. It means confronting neighbors when they try to prevent a Black or Brown person from moving into a community. It means cutting off ties with their racist parents if they don't change. It means losing people they love. However, they gain a sense of community with Black and Brown people as they use their white privilege to stand against racism.

Lecia Michelle writes and speaks about systemic racism so future generations will have a better chance at fulfilling their dreams. As a Black woman, she is passionate about the fight against racism and oppression. Knowing its effects firsthand, she is committed to its destruction. Giving up has never been an option.

THE CANCER THAT IS THE AMERICAN CRIMINAL JUSTICE SYSTEM

3

GLENN ROCESS

O N JULY 5TH, 1852, nearly a decade before Confederate artillery fired the first shots of the Civil War at Fort Sumter, escaped slave, social reformer, and orator Frederick Douglass stood before the Rochester (NY) Ladies' Anti-Slavery Society. He had spoken before the Society on several occasions, but this was to become the speech for which he is best remembered. Using the kind of high rhetoric no politicians have used in our own lifetimes, he described the perils, outrages, and travails enslaved people faced every day in slave states. One of the examples he used was that in Virginia, there were seventy-two crimes that were considered capital offenses for Black men, but only two that were capital offenses for white men.

One hundred sixty-five years later, the Booker Report on federal sentencing guidelines found that Black men still serve nearly twenty percent longer jail terms than do white men for similar crimes, and that nearly half the counties in Florida sentence Black citizens to more than double the jail time of white citizens for felony drug possession, even when their backgrounds are the same.

THE CANCER
THAT IS
AMERICA'S
CRIMINAL
JUSTICE
SYSTEM

The above paragraphs serve as proof positive of the systemic racism in our nation's government, of how "equal under the law" seems to be a Constitutional right for all but Black Americans. The more important consideration is exactly how and why this racism became so deeply ingrained in our law enforcement and judicial systems. The effects of societal and systemic racism—police brutality, minimum-sentencing requirements, and the undervaluing of Black victims by our judicial system—are repeatedly reinforced by the equally insidious effects of generational poverty and the growing political influence of for-profit prisons in local, state, and federal government.

POLICE BRUTALITY AND OVERPOLICING

This past summer, one name was heard more than any other: George Floyd, whose life was ended by a white Minneapolis policeman who kept his knee on Floyd's neck for eight minutes and forty-six seconds, long after Floyd had stopped responding. After a video of the murder was released to the public, mass protests were held not only in Minneapolis, but nationwide and around the world. Only then did most Americans begin hearing the names of Breonna Taylor, Stephon Clark, Elijah McClain, and so many other unarmed Black men and women who were murdered by police. The common thread found in each of these murders is overpolicing, wherein the police are too powerful, given too little oversight, and are not held to a higher standard of conduct. The confluence of those three factors in any organization leads unerringly to injustice, but in law enforcement, egregious misconduct and tragedy are inevitable.

GLENN
ROCESS

MINIMUM SENTENCING REQUIREMENTS

Perhaps the single most odious facet of the "War on Drugs" was the minimum sentencing requirements that became popular in the 1970s and 1980s. This resulted in the outrageous requirement that it would take possession of one hundred times the amount of powder cocaine versus crack cocaine to trigger the mandatory prison sentences. It was well-known at the time that crack cocaine was much more popular among Black people and that it would result in unconscionable racial disparities in sentencing, but the law was allowed to stand until 2010 when the standard was lowered to "only" eighteen-to-one. In 2018, the First Step Act decreased some of those minimum sentences, but only to a certain extent. The minimum sentencing requirements played a major role in the 800 percent growth of America's federal prison population between 1980 and 2015.

However well-intentioned minimum-sentencing laws may have been on the surface, the racist nature of their implementation has been nothing short of catastrophic for People of Color in general, and Black people in particular. The data clearly show whatever benefit these laws may have provided is more than negated by the damage done to the Black community as a whole. Such laws need to be stricken from the books at the first opportunity.

BAIL BONDS AND "JAIL CHURN"

THE CANCER
THAT IS
AMERICA'S
CRIMINAL
JUSTICE
SYSTEM

Every year, over 600,000 people enter prison gates, but people go to jail 10.6 million times each year. Jail churn is particularly high because most people in jails have not been convicted. Some have just been arrested and will make bail within hours or days, while many others are too poor to make bail and remain behind bars until their trial. Only a small number (about 160,000 on any given day) have been convicted and are generally serving misdemeanor sentences under a year.

The above finding by the Prison Policy Initiative illustrates one of the most troubling aspects of the American judicial system, of how strongly our courts are slanted against the poor. For those unfamiliar with the bail bond system, when a person is arrested, he or she may pay a certain amount of money to be held as a surety bond to guarantee the individual's appearance for trial at a later date. The amount of the bail bond is set (usually arbitrarily) by the judge at a bail hearing. If the individual doesn't appear, the bond is forfeited to the court. Bail bondsmen are private businesses that charge fees and interest for loans in the amount of bail set by the judge, sometimes for usurious rates. Interestingly enough, though its beginnings can be traced back to England in 1275, only the United States and the Philippines still use the bail bond system.

All too often, people are held in prison until trial simply because they can't afford bail without going deep in debt. As of 2018 in Texas, fully three-quarters of everyone in county jail were there because they could not make bail. Remember, every single one of these men and women—many (perhaps most) of whom were accused of nonviolent offenses—were still legally innocent as they sat in jail awaiting trial.

The particularly heinous result is that when such people are found completely innocent at trial, they will still have spent weeks and perhaps several months in jail for a crime they did not commit; and when they are released, they will likely have lost their jobs, meaning they and their families may be facing eviction from their homes. One tragic example is that of Kalief Browder, who spent three years imprisoned at Rikers Island in New York because he and his family could not afford the $3,000 needed for bail. He never went to trial—his charges were dropped due to lack of evidence, but he had still spent three years in state prison despite his innocence. He later took his ^own life.

The bail bond system was not originally designed to be racist, but because poverty in America weighs most heavily upon Black and Hispanic families, the bail bond system is certainly racist in effect. Some cities like New York and Atlanta have ended the cash bail system for those arrested for non-violent crimes, but for most of America, poverty can literally result in prison time.

THE CANCER
THAT IS
AMERICA'S
CRIMINAL
JUSTICE
SYSTEM

In 2016, Deputy Attorney General Sally Yates presented findings that a pool of fourteen privately operated federal prisons had higher rates of contraband, assault, and uses of force than did federally operated prisons, and that privately operated federal prisons did not save substantially on costs even though they generally provided fewer services. These were the justification for the Obama administration to direct the federal government to phase out use of privately operated prisons. Marc Mauer, executive director of The Sentencing Project, praised the move as a major milestone. He said, "It has been a stain on our democracy to permit profit-making entities to be handed the responsibility of making determinations of individual liberty."

Less then a year later, Attorney General Jeff Sessions of the Trump administration rescinded the order, saying it had "impaired the [Bureau of Prisons] ability to meet the future needs of the federal correctional system."

The main problem with Attorney General Sessions' claim is that it turned a blind eye to the fact that many privately run prisons negotiated contracts ensuring that they would be paid for at least 90 percent occupancy regardless of how many or how few people were incarcerated, thus giving privately operated prisons a vested financial interest in keeping its cells as fully occupied as possible. In Arizona, three such prisons negotiated contracts that guaranteed payments for 100 percent occupancy.

Even more troubling are the results of a study published by the *American Economic Journal* showing that prisoners remain in privately operated prisons from four to seven percent longer than in publicly operated prisons. The study states that one reason may be that the privately operated prisons have a financial interest in cutting costs, including by hiring less-experienced guards. The study found that inmates in privately run prisons were fifteen percent more likely to be given infractions, and those infractions are what parole boards use to consider when deciding whether to allow early release for good behavior.

As with bail bonds, the for-profit prison system was not designed to target minorities, but its overall effect is racist indeed. When convicts are sent to prisons that have fewer services, are less safe, and have guards who are often less professional and are more likely to hand out infractions, the privately operated prison system becomes directly responsible for increasing the recidivism rate of former inmates by as much as twenty percent. This effect is further magnified with minorities who are more likely to be sent to jail, and who are often given longer sentences than their white counterparts for similar crimes.

RACIAL VENGEANCE

A particularly troubling factor has been recently identified: racial vengeance. A study by the National Bureau of Economic Research found that even in vehicular homicides, a crime in which nearly all victims are random, sentencing for offenders who ended the lives of Black victims were fifty-three percent lower than the sentences for offenders whose victims were white. The difference is perversely reminiscent of the "Three-Fifths Compromise" at the 1787 Constitutional Convention wherein for every five slaves, only three were counted for representation in our federal government.

Whatever the reader may think of the disparity of the sentences between genders, there is no possible justification for this outrageous difference in sentences of perpetrators when compared to the races of their victims, as if the lives of the Black victims mattered little in the eyes of the courts. More than any of the other factors above, this one statistic validates the importance of and need for the Black Lives Matter movement.

THE CANCER
THAT IS
AMERICA'S
CRIMINAL
JUSTICE
SYSTEM

THE TUMOR FEEDING OUR NATION'S CANCER

America has five percent of the world's total population, but twenty percent of the world's prisoners. We have the world's largest prison population, both in terms of total inmates and of percentage of population. This shameful statistic is of our own making and is directly descended from the observation made by Frederick Douglass mentioned at the beginning of this article. We can see the evolution of our nation's racist judicial system from that day in 1852, through Reconstruction and the Jim Crow era, into the Civil Rights struggle, the Watts riots in 1965 and the Rodney King riots in 1992 (both of which were directly due to police brutality), to this summer's worldwide protests and several riots in reaction to multiple killings by police of unarmed Black men and women.

These murders are normally followed by deliberate inaction by law-enforcement agencies all too eager to sweep the incidents under the metaphorical rug until the public forgets about it. Even worse, there is still no database or system of tracking misconduct by police officers, meaning that if a police officer is fired for misconduct in one city, there's nothing stopping that officer from being hired in another city. Moreover, powerful police unions often fight tooth-and-nail to defend a police officer accused of misconduct no matter how damning the evidence is. In other words, police officers are effectively held to a lower standard of conduct (with lighter penalties) than are those whom they are sworn to serve and protect.

Looking at the above—and admittedly incomplete— list of racial disparities in America's judicial system, even one of the factors mentioned should by itself be an unconscionable scandal. But with so many factors, all woven so deeply into our nation's sociopolitical fabric, it is nothing short of miraculous that America's civil unrest hasn't seen a great deal more racial violence in every decade. If anything, Black Americans have shown a degree of patience and fortitude that only Job, who in the space of a day lost his children, his land, his belongings, and the love of his wife, might understand.

In his speech, Frederick Douglass described how deeply the self-inflicted harm of slavery was crippling America:

> *The existence of slavery in this country brands your republicanism as a sham, your humanity as a base pretence, and your Christianity as a lie. It destroys your moral power abroad; it corrupts your politicians at home. It saps the foundation of religion; it makes your name a hissing, and a byword to a mocking earth. It is the antagonistic force in your government, the only thing that seriously disturbs*

and endangers your Union. It fetters your prog-
ress; it is the enemy of improvement, the deadly foe
of education; it fosters pride; it breeds insolence; it
promotes vice; it shelters crime; it is a curse to the
earth that supports it; and yet, you cling to it, as if
it were the sheet anchor of all your hopes.

THE CANCER
THAT IS
AMERICA'S
CRIMINAL
JUSTICE
SYSTEM

Replace the fourth word in that paragraph—'slavery'—
with another word: racism. Then read the paragraph again.
The vice targeted by the paragraph would have changed,
but the accuracy and profundity thereof is changed not
at all. Douglass laid bare for all to see the clear and present danger that slavery posed to America as clearly as an
oncologist describing the deleterious effects of metas-
tasized cancer to all a body's organs to a frightened and
desperate patient.

With the change of that one word, his declaration rings
every bit as true today, for the cancer of racism still courses
through every artery and vein of our nation, ever replen-
ished and perpetuated by its original tumor in America's
judicial system. It is that malignancy that must be removed
first before we can have any real hope of surviving as a
nation, and as a people united, The healing must begin
with the judicial system.

Glenn Rocess is retired Navy, has traveled five continents, and has worn many hats, including as a steam plant supervisor, LAN admin, OSHA inspector, Foster parent of medically fragile children, and an adult family home owner. More importantly, he is a dad, a husband of twenty-eight years, and fears absolutely nothing except his wife's guilt trips.

THE SECRET LIVES OF BLACK WOMEN

4

MARLEY K

B EING A BLACK WOMAN in America can be a beautiful experience. There's nothing quite like being surrounded by powerful, classy, beautiful, sexy, sassy, fierce, smart, positive, and affirming Black women. I love our quick wit, our sassy mouths, and sense of style. There is also beauty in our diversity, which is reflected in women such as Sybrina Fulton, Mary J. Blige, Harriet Tubman, Diahann Carroll, Cicely Tyson, Oprah Winfrey, Hannah Drake, Danielle Moodie, Erykah Badu, Toni Morrison, Kitanya Harrison, Nina Simone, Ledisi, Coretta Scott and

Bernice King, Mo'Nique, Maya Angelou, Serena and Venus Williams, Michelle Obama, Queen Latifah, and so many others who exude the excellence, beauty, and charisma of Black women. We embody Black girl magic through our personal appearances, gifts, talents, and our undying spirits.

Beauty exists in the ways we express our love to one another. One thing I can count on in a group of sisters is a good laugh. I never laugh as hard as I do when I am in a room with random Black women. Good and grown Black sisters have an electric connection that I can't say I share with any other women on earth. The most beautiful thing about being a Black woman is how we revere one another. We understand the beauty of our unique struggle.

Life as a Black woman comes with many burdens. Being Black and a woman are two distinct but intertwined identities. No other people—no other women—in America are saddled with the unspoken and unrealistic expectations of carrying a nation and all its baggage for free, often suffering alone in silence. As a Black woman, we tend to everyone and everything before we tend to ourselves.

When I was a little girl, my mother told me on more than one occasion I was born with two strikes against me. I had no idea she meant being Black and a girl who would eventually grow into a Black woman . . . until I became of age and started working and living in the real world.

As a woman, I am born into a world full of people, but far too often I'm alone. Black women must be available to care for the needs of everyone, yet we are not fully accepted by everyone. It's a life of always being supportive, but rarely being supported. We are loved minimally if loved properly at all. I'm caring and compassionate, but somehow, we are the most emotionally neglected in the country.

The lives of many Black women are filled with never-ending expectations. In one moment we are presumed to be a savior, the source of healing for all in need; and in the next we are terrorized victims wondering when someone will save us. When does our redemption come? When can my Black self have a day of not alarming someone? Will I ever be loved with the compassion and nurturance with which I love others?

A burden of being a Black woman is knowing I am a descendant of enslaved people, human beings who were raped, tortured, and bred to make money for white people. The ramifications from our abuse and displacement live on in my people and throughout our communities today. How I am supposed to create healthy, whole people to help make America great when America never provided my people with the tools and resources to do so. Being a Black woman is living with generations of trauma.

MARLEY K

THE BURDEN OF HAVING BLACK SKIN

My Black skin puts me at a bigger disadvantage than other ethnic woman. Black women come into the world as Black girls who are told that nothing about us is good enough, but at the same time our lips, thighs, asses, and large breasts, and our pecan-tan skins are highly sought after.

Non-Black people have preconceived notions about us that we constantly must disprove. Black women must work twice as hard to be equal to white women. I work double-time to get and keep any job I have. It's extra work that I must perform simply to exist that I'm never paid for.

I have spent countless hours on a job cleaning up behind inept white saviors in the nonprofit sector, never realizing my white board members didn't value the expertise. Not only was I not paid any additional money for the hard work and extra hours worked, I was replaced with a new white woman after I cleaned up the mess from the last one.

Being a woman living in Black skin comes with the burden of having to prove that we are good mothers to our children because white supremacy has created the myth that we raise illiterate looters, killers, and rapists. Predictive policing and personal biases play a huge role in how rural kids are grouped. My son's elementary school kept countless Black children behind. Black children were disciplined differently. There was little tolerance for misbehaving Black youth compared to white students. All the disciplinarians were white men, which made many Black parents uncomfortable.

It became evident there were two tracks in the city's only elementary school: the track of success for white kids and the obstacle course of Black kids. The world demands that we demonstrate our intelligence because white supremacy mandates that my people are dumb and we perpetually breed dumb people. We must constantly prove that we are capable of leading. Society demands that we demonstrate beyond all doubt our value to society. Daily. Even as society neglects me and my Black children.

The burden of proof falls squarely on the backs of Black women to authenticate that we are capable of being a good steward of all that white America reigns over. The 2020 presidential candidacy of Senator Kamala Harris, despite her numerous qualifications and capabilities, highlighted just how hard Black women must work to prove to white people we are capable of being in charge. It felt like we were reliving President Obama's presidential candidacy. American white supremacy continues to show Black people that white people will always find ways to discount our capabilities and invalidate our accomplishments to maintain white people's perceptions, even if done subconsciously. If it's Black, it must prove it's good enough.

Despite warning white folks about potential bad voting decisions, Black women are seen as America's mammies and maids, and expected to clean up white messes and correct bad decisions made by white voters. But at the same time, we are not trusted to make the right decisions despite our collective track records proving otherwise, like Black women desperately begged America to not elect racists leaders who work to injure Black people and People of Color while running the nation into the ground. The nation ignored us. Now they expect us to clean up the mess in 2020. Black women are not America's standby maid.

I can outwork any woman of any nationality, yet I'm considered not good enough because my Black skin and Black birth name come with connotations pre-determined by people who have never met me. Being a Black woman means being hated due to hearsay. It's one of the reasons white people are afraid to ride the elevator with Black people. I call it the "Snowflake Effect." It's when white women or men get onto the elevator with "strange" people on it who they deem scary because they've been taught to fear Black folks. It means never being able to be all we can be because white supremacy and weaponized white feminism make sure we stay in our Black places at the end of the line.

Where there is Black skin there is no liberty, no justice, and for certain no peace. This is the definition of oppression.

THE BURDEN OF MY LIFE MATTERING LESS

Black women are treated as though our lives are valued less than any other women in America, despite being the most at-risk. When a Black woman or girl goes missing, the world doesn't stop to find her the way it does to find a white woman or girl with blond hair or an Asian coed. Being a Black woman comes with the realization that my life and the life of anyone birthed by me does not matter.

Unlike when white women are killed, when my Black sisters are killed by our spouses, partners, significant others, or complete strangers it barely makes the news. Instead, the world treats us as if we somehow deserved it. According to the National Center on Violence Against Black Women in the Black Community, African American women and girls twelve years old and older experienced higher rates of rape and sexual assault than white, Asian, and Latina girls and women between 2005 and 2010, yet white women and girls get all the attention and urgency.

Black woman aren't taken seriously by physicians when we're in pain or when we tell them something is wrong with our bodies. According to statistics from the U.S. Office of Minority Health's 2017 Infant Mortality Statistics from the 2017 Period Linked Birth/Infant Death Data Set, across all socioeconomic statuses, Black women are about three times more likely than white women to die from preventable birth-related complications. Black women are not being helped by people in positions to help us because our Black bodies matter less to them. How long will Black women, who are required to be superwomen every day of our lives, continue to receive substandard medical attention compared to that of white women?

I watch non-Black feminists espouse how we intersect in various ways such as through race, class, and gender, yet they sit and apathetically watch as the police disrespect and mop Waffle House floors with their so-called sisters in the struggle, like Chikesia Clemons, or are killed by police while in their homes asleep, like my sister Breonna Taylor. The support of these intersectionality frauds is absent without leave as we are called derogatory names in public by white and white Hispanic men. Our fair-weather sisters in arms often stand by and watch others verbally harass us while working or shopping. I know wherever I am in this world, I am viewed as less than.

MARLEY K

THE BURDEN OF SIMPLY BEING

I can't speak my truth because it's never enough for white people. As a Black woman, my natural hair is a burden, my dark skin is a burden, my tone is a burden, my style is a burden, my passion is a burden, my words are a burden, the shape of my body is a burden, and my spirit is a burden. Being a Black woman means at any time I'm an annoyance to folks for no other reason than I exist. The burden of a Black woman is feeling emotional and having to sit with our emotions for fear of living up to the stereotypes of white folks and many Black men about "angry" Black women.

49

There is a lot to love about being a Black woman. The thing I love most about being a Black woman is finally growing into myself. I love my body, personality, attitude, style, and my mind now, and I have enjoyed the journey getting here—not because it was easy but because it helped to shape my character. Learning to love me has been quite the journey, but I've finally arrived. Once I stopped living for the world and was able to discover who I was, I was

able to set myself free, released from the invisible chains that bound me. No longer am I tied to beauty standards not made for me, nor a world not ready for me. Good, kind, Black women helped mold and shape me into the Black woman I have become, and for that, I am eternally grateful. Parts of them live inside of me. They are my sisters from another mother. Because of them, I now stand.

Black women rock. We are magical and yet somehow mysterious. How is it that we are able to carry our burdens and still rise? Black women are goddesses, queens, and diamonds. My Black sisters and I are priceless. We know our worth, and for the first time in a long time we understand our value. The world knows our value and they hate us for it. The world could not run without us and could not be without us. That's why I love us so much. Being a Black woman is complex, special, beautiful, and at times a burden, and I wouldn't trade any of it for the world.

Marley K writes articles on Medium.com that focus on race, equality, government, politics, policy, life lessons, anti-racism, and current events. Her articles are on e-zine sites including *Level, ZORA, Our Human Family,* and *Age of Awareness.* She contributes articles about race relations in America as well as understanding and dismantling white supremacy. Her articles balance information mixed with hard truths. Read more by visiting her blog at Medium.com/@MarleyK.

THE CONSTRUCT OF WHITENESS

THE ORIGINS OF WHITENESS 5

WILLIAM SPIVEY

D EFINING WHITENESS IS LIKE defining air: it is all
around, you are so accustomed to its existence that
you mostly pay no attention to it except on a particularly
windy day. It is typically benign, but during a tornado
or hurricane it can cause considerable damage or death.
Whiteness is usually unnoticed; in America it is the status quo. Whiteness is taken for granted, it is the baseline,
whiteness just is.

If there is one thing you should know about whiteness,
it is this: Whiteness is not inherited, it is learned. There are

no inherent characteristics, and whiteness cannot exist in a vacuum. Whiteness is a trait solely dependent on interaction with other people, whether they be People of Color or other white people. Whiteness can be an attitude, a set of beliefs; sometimes, it presents itself through group consciousness or individual conclusions. Though often influenced by the environment one grows up in, whiteness is not inherited, it is learned.

Little children have no concept of whiteness until they are trained to heed it. While they may have some curiosity about differences in color, it is not until someone supplies them with a reason for those differences that judgment occurs. That reason may or may not have any basis, but a belief system begins all the same.

Whiteness is embedded in American history: the first colonists, the founders, those that compiled our laws and developed our policies, did so with whiteness in mind. The Constitution never explicitly mentions race, yet its Articles are filled with provisions to constrain. Article 1, Section 9 provided that Congress would continue to permit the "migration or importation of such persons as any of the States now existing shall think proper to admit," for at least twenty years. Translated, it said that Congress could not block the importation of enslaved people because slaveholding states needed them for their economy. The plan was never to end slavery after twenty years but to replace enslaved people from other countries with home-grown domestic enslaved people, often the result of forced breeding or rape. Slave labor camps (plantations) also served as breeding farms; at a time when tobacco was depleting the nutrients in the soil in Virginia, Maryland, and other states, they turned to another crop—enslaved people that they sent further south and west which soon became Virginia's leading export.

The Electoral College is established in Article II, Section 1; it is a mechanism that kept the less populous slave-holding states from being outvoted by the other states to outlaw slavery. While technically the slave states may have had more people, the enslaved themselves were unable to vote even though they were counted as three-fifths of a person for the purpose of Congressional representation. The Electoral College was a check against the pure will of the people to attain a more predictable result. It is how we get presidents who lose the popular vote yet reflect the will of the less populous, mostly white states.

WILLIAM SPIVEY

America's borders reflect whiteness. To the north, the Canadian border is the result of white countries dividing up land between themselves that was not theirs. When expanding westward, America adopted "Manifest Destiny," the position that God directed America to take possession of all land extending to the Pacific Ocean (later amended to include Hawaii and in some minds the Philippines). Senator Albert J. Beveridge said it most clearly in 1900: "God has not been preparing the English-speaking and Teutonic peoples for a thousand years for nothing but vain and idle self-admiration. No! He has made us the master organizers of the world to establish a system where chaos reigns . . . He has made us adept in government that we may administer government among savages and senile peoples." To be clear, when Beveridge said "English-speaking" and "Teutonic peoples," he meant white.

America's expansion also caused southern considerations when it came to Texas and Mexico. There was great debate about how much of what was Mexico to take into our Union. The problem with absorbing too much of Mexico was too many Mexicans. South Carolina Senator John C. Calhoun, whose towering statue was only recently removed from its Charleston, South Carolina perch, said this in a January 4, 1848 speech to Congress: "We have conquered many of the neighboring tribes of Indians, but we have never thought of holding them in subjection, or of incorporating them into our Union. They have been left as an independent people in the midst of us or have been driven back into the forests. Nor have we ever incorporated into the Union any but the Caucasian race. To incorporate Mexico, would be the first departure of the kind; for more than half of its population are pure Indians, and by far the larger portion of the residue mixed blood. I protest against the incorporation of such a people. Ours is the Government of the white man. The great misfortune of what was formerly Spanish America, is to be traced to the fatal error of placing the Colored race on an equality with the white." History shows us the essence of American whiteness, that the nation is, of, and for white people. And it is ordained by God.

If only whiteness were something relegated to the past. One of the arguments whiteness uses as a defense is that the racially repugnant aspects of it ended after the Civil War, or the Civil Rights Acts, or the Voter Rights Act. Most people are not aware that throughout American history, there have been multiple civil and voter rights acts, and each and every one has ultimately been rejected, limited in scope, or found wholly or partially unconstitutional by the Supreme Court, whose primary purpose is to interpret laws according to the Constitution. The Constitution that was established to protect white interests, specifically the interests of white, male, landowners.

Whiteness and maleness have much in common but that will remain a subject for another day. Whiteness has had a staunch protector in the Supreme Court that constantly requires the justices to consider the "intent of the Founders," as the basis for their rulings. Whiteness is propped up by the courts, Congress, and our schools who teach revisionist history and make heroes out of heathens. Many of our schools mandate "American exceptionalism" be taught; students pledge allegiance to a flag and Republic that has always favored its white citizens more. American exceptionalism is thinly veiled white exceptionalism, especially when taken in the context used. Whiteness is like the air, it is everywhere.

In defining whiteness, it is important to understand what whiteness is not. The Smithsonian National Museum of African American History and Culture recently issued guidelines for talking about race. One of their graphics discussed "Aspects and Assumptions of Whiteness in the United States." It said white values included "rational thinking," and "hard work." White people were also assumed to "put hard work before play," utilize "objective, rational, linear thinking," and apply "quantitative emphasis," among other traits. When asked to comment, the museum declined and removed the graphic from their website. Something that still stands and is inarguably correct is the following, from the same source: "White dominant culture, or whiteness, refers to the ways white people and their traditions, attitudes, and ways of life have been normalized over time and are now considered standard practices in the United States [...] And since white people still hold most of the institutional power in America, we have all internalized some aspects of white culture—including People of Color."

Whiteness demands that children of all minorities learn to talk white, act white, and even think white to fit in. Except for one month a year, we are taught white history from a white perspective. Historical figures are white-washed, and we are rarely informed of their mistreatment of enslaved people, broken treaties with Native Americans, abuse of Asian railroad workers, and no more than a brief mention of Japanese internment camps. Every institution is designed to promote the message that white is right, which gets to the heart of the matter of what whiteness is.

The one thing you were asked to remember about whiteness is that it is learned, and therefore, it can be unlearned. The belief of white superiority is at the core of white supremacist groups, and most white racist behavior. I disagree with the premise that only white people can be racist, that trait can exist in all races. Systemic racism, however; can be attributed only to those who control and design the system, which in America leaves white people standing alone. Because white people control the system, they must be part of the solution to rooting out the beliefs attached to whiteness. And those not part of the solution, are part of the problem.

As ubiquitous as whiteness is, a high percentage of white people at least claim to be unaware of the problem.

These are the white people who "don't see color" or believe racism ended long ago. They are blissfully unaware of the history that has granted them general economic advantages that were given and not earned. They may know that the G.I. Bill helped establish the middle class by creating a path to homeownership for veterans. Homeownership for most families greatly increased their net worth and in some cases over time led to generational wealth. What they missed was that the G.I. Bill was almost universally denied to Black veterans; even when determined eligible, lenders stood in their way to keep them from taking advantage of homeownership. Whiteness does not require acknowledgement of how things came to be. Whiteness often teaches that being white makes one entitled to certain privileges and, conversely, not being white may be a disqualification. But whiteness can be overcome, just as it can be unlearned.

WILLIAM SPIVEY

The first part of unlearning whiteness is a strong dose of truth—not just for white people because all Americans have been fed the same misinformation. The purpose of teaching the truth about how America came to be is not to induce shame or guilt, but to promote a true understanding of how things came to be and that other people were denied opportunities reserved for whites alone. At least some of the newly enlightened will recognize the need to strive for equality and understand that doing nothing is not really doing nothing but helping to maintain the status quo—and whiteness is the status quo.

There are those always seeking to dialog or begin having conversation on the subject as if talking alone is a cure. The steps to eradicate whiteness include erasing the laws and policies that support it. If we do not accept the challenge of a total overhaul of the present system, then we can at least work within it to require change. It means taking the time to vet people before electing them and not rewarding intransigence with an additional term. We should require that our elected officials work together instead of just saying no. The Senate should perform its role to advise and consent in confirmation hearings as opposed to simply following party lines. The current process gives us judges selected on their ideological views as opposed to their ability to fairly apply the law. A nominee that relies on "original intent" should be immediately rejected as the original intent of the Constitution promoted whiteness.

The Supreme Court should no longer be allowed to do its work behind closed doors. Part of their ability to construct decisions that uphold whiteness is their ability to ironically do what they do in the dark. Oral arguments should be televised like other courtrooms so that excesses can be exposed. I support justices having to face questions about their decisions as do politicians and other judges without lifetime appointments.

Voter suppression must be eliminated. Republicans are doing now what Democrats did earlier. Each has quashed minority voting when it served their needs and always to support whiteness. Voter suppression is not simply requiring a photo identification to vote (although it can be). It is making polling places inconvenient for minority populations to access or creating four- to six-hour-long lines in urban locations. It is reducing early voting days and times; it is creating unconstitutional poll taxes as another barrier to placing a vote. It is gerrymandering and redistricting and any other method designed to produce a result other than the will of the people.

Whiteness is not inherited, it is learned. It is however influenced by peer pressure, one's environment, and one's willingness to acknowledge its existence. Even acknowledgement is not the cure. Whiteness is dependent on most of those who recognize it, doing nothing to stop it. Irish statesman Edmund Burke is credited with saying, "The only thing necessary for the triumph of evil is for good men to do nothing." But that is not all he said. He added, "When bad men combine, the good must associate; else they will fall, one by one, an unpitied sacrifice in a contemptible struggle." It will take good men and women of all colors to eliminate whiteness, because the bad men have already combined.

Whiteness is not inherited, it is learned. It is also a choice that can be walked away from at any time. Like quitting smoking, it is never too late to benefit from stopping a bad habit that is hurting you. Whiteness is not the same as being white. There is nothing wrong with being white or any other color. The harm comes from believing that whiteness includes superiority and entitlement. That is what must be ended.

There is one last thing to consider, "What happens when the construct of whiteness is gone?" Nature abhors a vacuum and when the construct of whiteness is eradicated, it follows something will take its place. That something need not be equally unpalatable based on the same paradigm. Let constructs rooted in equality, kindness, and respect take their place.

Instituting these values cannot be government mandates and they don't need a large group to begin. Let each of us open our hearts and minds and try to see our neighbors, friends, co-workers, and strangers as more than their color. Making the world a better place starts with making your neighborhood, school, or workplace better. It begins with each of us, tossing aside the remnants of whiteness and implementing a philosophy based on oneness in its stead.

Oneness is a far better principle to use as a belief system. Where inequality exists, look for a solution that promotes oneness to rectify the situation. Oneness implies fairness which is hard to argue against as something any group of people deserves.

One last word to anyone who seems either knowingly or unknowingly clinging to whiteness and white supremacy. The two are unsustainable models and demographics are not on their side. Recent estimates project white people will become a minority in America by the year 2045. Perpetuating these paradigms while in the minority will no doubt prove problematic. Implementing inclusive rather than exclusive schema will be a better way forward for us all.

William Spivey resides in Orlando, Florida and has a Bachelor of Arts in Economics from Fisk University. He who was once just a basketball player, transformed himself to a historian and writer because that is what was required. He also has eight grandchildren—all girls. "The more important the task, the easier it is to focus."

THE FREEDOM TO BE: DEFINING WHITE PRIVILEGE AND WHITE SUPREMACY

6

JOHN METTA

I HAD A CRUSH on a girl named Tamika when I was in fifth grade. Tamika could light a whole room with her smile and high-pitched, hiccup laugh. I was a poetry-loving geek, and more than once, I was kept from a beating by this fearless protector of the weak. She was powerful, but most of that power was kindness.

Tamika had a scar on the inside of her left knee that was shaped like a crescent moon and I used to watch mesmerized as her hand rested on her lap, finger lightly tracing that moon back and forth, back and forth. Sometimes,

Tamika would leave school early to be with her mom at work and I imagined going with her.

There's a sound that still causes me to remember her. It's the sound of a beaded entry way, or certain wooden wind chimes. The sound of the beads at the ends of Tamika's cornrows, clicking softly as she moved.

Seeing Tamika was the highlight of my day, but one day, I went to school and she was just . . . gone.

I thought she was sick, but after three days I became convinced I would never see her smile again, or hear the sound of her cornrows quietly clicking as we talked to one another. When I asked my teacher about her, she simply grimaced and told me to go back to my seat.

. . .

On May 30, 1975, Toni Morrison gave a talk at Portland State University titled "A Humanist's View." She began by detailing the language used to describe early American economics, reading from a book entitled *The Historical Statistics of the United States from Colonial Times to 1957*—"which documents," she stated, "in chronological order and by point of destination of import and export, those humans who came to the United States from 1619-1769."

In her speech, she noted that we have generations of scientific study and economic analysis that documents us, the children of Africa's diaspora, as if we were not people at all. "No group has had more money spent on it to have its genetics examined, its fecundity stopped, its intelligence measured" by "people who know our sperm count, but they don't know our names."

We Black Americans are beset by statistics. Numbers, not culture, often describe us as Americans.

- 69%: Nationwide average of Black students graduating high school, 20% lower than their white counterparts.
- 33%: Percentage of Black men who will be imprisoned in their lifetime.
- 10%: Percentage of Black ownership in a neighborhood before housing prices fall.

Statistics have defined us since the times when the greatest care was taken to detail the "Number of Negroes Shipped." But, as Morrison noted, those statistics are without names. They are numbers without stories, facts disconnected from the people who fight and suffer.

"Pretty much like the historical statistics is Black American history," Morrison stated, "a separate book, a separate chapter, or a separate section of origins and consequences of slavery, all of which is related to production and legislature, very seldom to the very fabric of life and culture in this country."

There is an irony, then, that when we talk about what it means to be Black in America, we ourselves so often fall back on the statistics that define us. Number of us who have died at the hands of the police, or people acting like police. Percentage of us who graduate high school, or who don't survive it. Studies showing our intelligence is equal to those of European descent, that our educational opportunities are both limited and focused on punishment and incarceration.

JOHN
METTA

• • •

I met Tamika again only once. It was years later in high school when I recognized her hiccup laugh from across the room. We were setting up for a debate team competition between her school and mine, and when she saw me her face broke into that sunshine smile.

"It's so good to see you!" She said. "I knew you'd do something like this, you were always reading all those books."

We were both the captains of our school's debate teams and I told her I was happy to debate on the side against capital punishment because it's really what I believe.

"I don't believe in capital punishment either," she said, then she smiled. "But this isn't about what I believe, it's about winning—so I'm going to destroy you."

And she did. Tearing down every argument we made against capital punishment like the goddess Oya tearing down trees with her hurricane breath.

After the event, we had time to talk and she told me why she moved to a different school.

"My mama got into a fight with that principal one too many times."

It turns out Tamika never left school early to spend time with her mother at work. Rather, she had routinely been sent home by school administration because her hair was "inappropriate and distracting."

• • •

It is impossible to describe white supremacy without a detailed accounting of what it means to be a Black person in America. "To define Black people," as Morrison warned, "as reactions to white presence."

We are forced to document our culture, our biology,

our language not as aspects of our own, which have merit in and of themselves, but as contrasted to the expectations of white America. Even the language we use is white. Words, grammar, and sentence cadence forced upon us with neither relation to nor acceptance of our West African heritage.

It is a privilege, you see, to define oneself on one's own terms, in one's own language, without even a thought for the existence of another culture. We do not share that privilege. We pour ink onto pages proclaiming our right to exist and in doing so become mere marks set against the background of paper; having a message and meaning, perhaps, but no form without the whiteness of the page to define us. The page, by contrast, exists whether our ink marks it or not.

We, the black marks set against this white page, are forced to consider the paper. What is the shape on which we are written? What form does the pulp take that forces the ink of our existence to smear and skip as we document ourselves against its background?

While it is not a complete picture, this is often how I describe the concept of white privilege. White people have the freedom to be. Not the freedom to be any particular thing, mind you, but the freedom merely to exist at all, without consideration for where and how they are allowed to do so. (Footnote: This is a necessarily limited view of privilege because of the topic of this book. I frequently note that similar arguments can rightfully be made regarding my male privilege by women, my cis privilege by LGBTQ people, and so on. This description is not meant to limit the discussion, but rather to focus it in this setting.) By contrast, Black people only are something in relation to whiteness. Our entire existence is defined by how we fit (or too often do not fit) into American—white European—culture.

Three moments in history help to illustrate this.

. . .

In the year 1066, Norman France invaded Anglo-Saxon England and forcibly changed their language. The destruction of a conquered people's language is a useful tool of oppression. So after their invasion, Normans cemented power by making French the official language of the state, and even outlawed English in some cases. (Footnote: I am using "French" and "English" here for simplicity. For the strict definitions and linguistic history of Anglo-Norman and Anglo-Saxon, consult any decent history book.) The strategy was so successful that the English speakers themselves began to associate the French language with sophistication and their own English language and culture with vulgarity.

Now it is important to note that William The Conquerer did not believe the English were inferior to the French. Not in any real sense. The portrayal of the English as inferior and the denouncement of their language and culture was only and entirely done to justify their domination. Convincing a people of their own worthlessness is a powerful way to support the structures of economic domination.

It is important we realize this was done simply to dominate, but was so effective that the dominated people believed it themselves and one thousand years later still do. We still hold French at a higher linguistic register than English, considering French customs more "refined" than Anglo-Saxon. To this day, we smile at a "scent" but wrinkle our noses at a "smell," we "eat" at a BBQ but "dine" at a fancy restaurant. The structures that supported economic oppression ten centuries ago have become as much a part of our own culture as the pulp of the paper on which we write our history.

Centuries later, similar tools were used during the early years of our country when Africans were brought here as chattel and portrayed as animals. Enslaved men, women, and children were beaten for speaking their own language, beaten for learning to read and write, beaten for walking without proof of passage, beaten merely for not answering to a white man like a trained dog. And this control was enforced by slave patrols. In many places, service in slave patrols was compulsory for all white men. What better way to ensure that a particular portrayal of Black people would become embedded into society than to ensure every white citizen was forced to participate in it?

JOHN
METTA

Much like the Norman subjugation of English culture, slavery and its history was never about the inferiority of Black people. As Morrison so eloquently noted in her speech, it was about economics and power. "Why increase the sons of Africa by planting them in America," Benjamin Franklin noted, "where we have so fair an opportunity by excluding all the Blacks and Tawneys." And much like Norman France, the language of oppression became part of our culture and belief. "I entirely agree with you," wrote Theodore Roosevelt, "that as a race and in the mass, the Negroes are altogether inferior to white people."

"Nobody really thought that Black people were inferior." Morrison notes. "Not Benjamin Franklin, not Mr. Byrd, and not Theodore Roosevelt. They only hoped that they would behave that way."

Convincing a people of their own worthlessness is a powerful way to support the structures of economic domination.

The portrayal of Black and Brown people as dangerous, as lazy, as animalistic is so embedded in our culture that, much like dining versus eating, Black people even use the language ourselves. We can see this in an Op Ed by a Black writer in The Independent titled "Charleston shooting: Black and Muslim killers are 'terrorists' and 'thugs.' Why are white shooters called 'mentally ill'?"

Did you catch that? Black and Muslim people are "killers" while white people are merely "shooters." Even when we talk about the different language used to describe Black and Brown people, we use coded racist language to do it.

The very shape of the paper on which we write our own story is the shape of white domination.

When I consider this history, I ask certain questions. White America can cling to even accidental culture such as "eating" vs "dining" for over a thousand years. Why should we expect Black people to lose the culture of West Africa after only a few generations if not because we find that culture less valid than European culture?

More to the point, if we still cling to the artificial prejudices of the French from a thousand years ago, what hope do we have of destroying the prejudices of slavers in our own lifetimes?

• • •

White supremacy and white privilege, like electricity and magnetism, are two manifestations of the same force. Wrap an electrical wire around a core of iron and you cannot help but generate a magnetic field that attracts metals that are aligned properly while it repels others. When we wrap white culture around the core—the belief that it is "normal"— we can't help but generate its sibling force, the privilege to know that whiteness is properly aligned, and all others will be repelled.

This is white supremacy. Not so much belief that white European culture is better, as the unconscious acceptance that white European culture is normal. White privilege is the ability to exist within that norm, pulled forward by its magnetism rather than repelled by its invisible force. This is no better illustrated than by the hair of Black women.

White people are allowed the freedom to let their hair simply grow. By contrast, the very biology of Black women is regulated. A Black woman simply allowing her hair to grow is so disturbing to white America that it can only be seen as a political statement. It would be no less revolutionary today than it was when Angela Davis arrived in court in 1971.

- 80%: Percentage of Black women who modify their natural hair to fit into a corporate workspace.

Tamika, whose hair was controlled by a style that existed before Europeans existed, was removed from school for hair that was called "distracting." Yet without braids, she was just as likely to be removed from school, as so many young girls have, because her hair was "unkempt." Whatever Tamika did, she could be labeled as "wrong."

JOHN
METTA

75

The reason was not Tamika's hair, it was that convincing a people of their own worthlessness is a powerful way to support the structures of economic domination. The very biology of Blackness has always been legislated. From Black procreation to Black presence in white spaces to the acceptability of Black hair.

On July 3, 2019, California became the first state to pass the Crown Act, a law preventing discrimination against natural hair and protective hair styles in schools and offices. Some mark this as a triumph, I cannot see why. We have embedded the language of white supremacy so deeply in our culture that in the 21st century we cannot even accept the basic biology of Black people without legislative action. How, I wonder, can white people not see the need for the Crown Act as anything but embarrassing?

DEFINING
WHITE
PRIVILEGE
AND WHITE
SUPREMACY

· · ·

"AN ACT *to enforce the constitutional right to vote, to confer jurisdiction upon the district courts of the United States to provide injunctive relief against discrimination in public accommodations, to authorize the Attorney General to institute suits to protect constitutional rights in public facilities and public education, to extend the Commission on Civil Rights, to prevent discrimination in federally assisted programs, to establish a Commission on Equal Employment Opportunity, and for other purposes.*"

The first paragraph of the Civil Rights Act of 1964, reads as if it is "the most sweeping civil rights legislation since

Reconstruction." Yet in the time since, we have been set by statistics.

- 6.5%: 2018 national unemployment rate for Black Americans, over twice as high as that for white Americans.

"It's important, therefore, to know who the real enemy is," Morrison wrote in her 1975 speech, "and to know the function, the very serious function of racism, which is distraction. It keeps you from doing your work. It keeps you explaining over and over again, your reason for being. Somebody says you have no language and so you spend 20 years proving that you do. Somebody says your head isn't shaped properly so you have scientists working on the fact that it is. Somebody says that you have no art so you dredge that up. Somebody says that you have no kingdoms and so you dredge that up."

Somebody says your hair is inappropriate and distracting, so you dredge that up. But a hair law will not enforce equality any more than the Civil Rights Act did. Black women's hair is protected, so it'll be their tone of voice, or their walk, or their clothes. It is not about hair, or about color, or about gender. As Morrison put it, "there will always be one more thing," because "the disease is not racism. It is greed and the struggle for power."

• • •

Years ago, when social media was still new, I stumbled upon Tamika's Facebook page.

She had just announced her partnership in a small law firm fighting against Black incarceration and I saw a

JOHN
METTA

77

picture of her magical smile, matched by her daughter's. I never connected with her, that whole scene of connecting with everyone you ever knew never sat well with me, but I did read a couple entries on her blog and learned a bit about her life.

She wrote one post on why she got her law degree. Too many Black men, she wrote, die in prison. Men like her husband, a promising college student picked up for suspicion of drug possession whose life was then forfeit.

Another post was about her hair. Like so many Black women, she chose to straighten her hair and get a "more womanly" hairstyle as a way to appear "more professional" in court. She wrote that she believed in Black women's right to wear whatever hair style they wanted, but chose the step because she knew she had to in order to be taken seriously in court. Tamika fought her own biology to give her defendants the best chance at fighting for freedom against crimes they often did not even commit. Convincing a people of their own worthlessness is a powerful way to support the structures of economic domination.

John Metta has degrees in Geology, Anthropology, Geography, and Ecological Engineering. He served in the Army during Desert Storm as a surgical technician and the Navy as a submariner. A lover of learning, he has worked as a cook, underwater archaeologist, hydrologist, and software engineer. He lives in Oregon with his wife, children, and pet fountain pen.

EDUCATING BLACK STUDENTS IN WHITE SPACES

7

CHARLES WHITE

From 1619 until the end of slavery, enslaved Black people were denied access to education. If a Black person was caught learning how to read and write, they would be immediately sold to another plantation or whipped. The white people in the Antebellum (pre-Civil War) South knew that once Black people possessed education and could read the United States Constitution and the Declaration of Independence, then the idea of slavery would become hypocritical. How do you say all men are created equal, but in the same breath, state

Black people are less than human and don't deserve the same rights?

White spaces—places where Black people are marginalized—are filled with traps and pitfalls to keep the Black person under the thumb of white supremacy. It's an insidious monster that cripples Black people with poverty and a lack of opportunity. We are marginalized in the white power structure. We are not given the same opportunities as other members of this so-called equal nation.

White spaces and ideologies about the Black people in those spaces are why police kill African Americans at a higher rate than their white counterparts. The poverty rate among Black families is over twenty percent, according to several charts recently released by CNN, whereas white poverty is just over eight percent. The same report speaks on a homeownership rate of forty-four percent among the Black community, whereas nearly seventy-four percent of white people own their homes. Furthermore, eighteen percent of Black home loan applications are denied, locking them out of a critical means to build generational wealth.

In our nation's schools, Black students are ignored and allowed to fall through the cracks. They are treated as insignificant or ignored in the white space of education. How can one ever be equal in an education system that overlooks one of the greatest humanitarian crises in American history: American slavery. The effect is that Black children don't know their own history. I've spoken to kids who believe slavery ended in the 1950s. One child was

EDUCATING BLACK STUDENTS IN WHITE SPACES

82

under the impression his grandmother had been enslaved and picked cotton.

THE ORIGINS OF JIM CROW

In 1896, the infamous *Plessy v. Ferguson* case decision drastically changed the lives of Black Americans. The United States Supreme Court authorized Jim Crow as the law of the land in the South. The phrase "separate but equal" was made popular that year and laid the bedrock for a racist system that devoured Black lives like a starved monster.

CHARLES
WHITE

The case was simple. A Black man named Homer Plessy wanted to sit in the front of a streetcar in New Orleans, but the city's Separate Car Act prevented a Black person from doing so. Homer willfully violated this law. After losing in the lower court, the Supreme Court heard the case. A majority opinion ruled that separate but equal did not violate the Fourteenth Amendment, which provides equal protection under the law regardless of race. At that juncture, white spaces became off-limits to millions of Black people living in the South.

This situation lasted until another Supreme Court case in 1954 overturned separate but equal. *Brown v. Board of Education* is one of the most important civil rights cases in American history. This case made segregation based on race illegal in all schools across the nation. At that moment, the Court's previous decision became invalid, and white spaces in education were open to integration.

The Supreme Court stated in their decision that with all deliberate speed schools must be desegregated, and

African Americans integrated into the nation's public and private schools.

The nation was not ready for integration. Once Black kids began to enter a school system that was rigged against them because of bias and racism, we began to see achievement gaps, low graduation rates, and high suspension numbers. According to John B. King, of The Education Trust, the education of Black students has been named the new frontline for civil rights.

EDUCATIONAL SPACES
DO NOT REFLECT THE STUDENT BODY

According to the Economic Policy Institute, Black students are five times more likely to attend a segregated school than their white counterparts. Why? Because Black people of lower incomes tend to live in the same community. Over the last several decades, schools have become less integrated. Furthermore, Black students who attend a mostly poor and Black school do not perform well on standardized tests.

The vast majority of the nation's teaching force is white, and even in a school with a significant minority population, most of the teaching staff are white women. In my school district, sixty-seven percent of the kids are minorities, while over eighty-five percent of the teachers are white. Only four percent of the teachers in my school district are Black. There is no active recruitment of Black teachers in my district. Furthermore, teachers of Color are fired on a more regular basis.

White and Black kids perform better when taught by a

more diverse workforce. The teaching force should reflect the school population. These individuals are role models to our kids and provide an example of a successful person who looks like them. Furthermore, teachers of Color have experiences similar to the populations they teach. They understand racism and how it affects minority children. And in many cases, a Black child feels more comfortable speaking to a Black teacher or administrator.

In my career as a school administrator and now as a teacher at the local juvenile detention center, I find that African American children open up more to me. They explain in detail their fears and aspirations. The white space is tough on our minority kids and they feel marginalized every day they attend a classroom in their zoned school.

Furthermore, the curriculum Black students are taught in school is severely whitewashed. African American history is a blip on the curriculum radar screen. Students are not taught the greatness of Black Africans or African Americans. Heroes like Nat Turner, Denmark Vessy, and Toussaint L'Overture are readily ignored. We had a history before slavery, but in our public schools, Black people are treated as if we never existed before arriving in this country.

CHARLES
WHITE

THE MARGINALIZATION OF BLACK STUDENTS

It is unfortunate that once Black kids enter white schools or schools with predominately white teaching staff and administration, fairness in discipline can become an issue. A recent study conducted by two doctoral students at the

University of California Berkley found that Black kids are suspended at a rate four times higher than whites.

Kids who are suspended often are more likely to go to jail. Furthermore, they do not complete high school. In the juvenile detention center where I work, about eighty percent of the students are not in school. I remember a young man who had not been to school in for two years. He was fifteen years old. When asked why he did not go to school, he said there was no value in education, and the teachers did not want to help him. I find this to be the case with a vast majority of the kids I teach.

Over the years, I've seen kids suspended from school for not bringing a pencil to class. It can be something as minor as an argument with a teacher that leads to multiple days at home. While these children are suspended, the parent is usually at work. The child has absolutely no supervision and usually finds trouble on the streets of their communities. Poverty takes a significant toll on my students. The majority of them reside in single-parent homes with multiple children. When I ask why they commit crimes on the street, most of the time it is a matter of survival.

Implicit bias is a real problem amongst teachers and administrators in our nation's schools. It is the reason so many Black kids are suspended and excessively disciplined. Some white teachers do not understand why Black students act out in the classroom. Children of all races act up in class, but usually the white student receives a lesser punishment than the Black student for the same offense.

If a teacher took the time to build a relationship with a child and ask questions, the classroom issues would significantly decrease. Several years ago, when I was an assistant principal at a local school, many students approached me in the hall. They were visibly upset. I asked what was wrong, and they explained to me that the teacher told them they would be on welfare in a few years and pregnant. The hurt and anger in their eyes was heartbreaking. They trusted this white teacher to teach them without bias and did not expect this type of treatment.

Situations like the one above frustrate Black students and can lead to them dropping out. They do not feel welcome in the white space of education and would instead pursue a GED if possible. Way too many children go to jail for years because of multiple expulsions at the hands of out-of-touch administrators who continue to feed the school-to-prison pipeline.

CHARLES WHITE

In essence, the school to prison pipeline is a systemic practice of pushing Black kids out of schools due to expulsions and suspensions. This puts the students in contact with law enforcement and leads to incarceration at an early age. I see this ugly phenomenon each day at my job teaching youth in the detention center. I ask my students how many have been suspended multiple times, and the majority raise their hands. Several have been expelled from school twice for up to two years at a time. How can a child expect to escape the jaws of incarceration when they are never in school, earning an education. This is once again white supremacy raising its head in the white space of American schools. Education is a great equalizer. It doesn't cure the problems of racism in this country, but it does give a Black child a leg up in the fight.

It is not uncommon for Black parents to mistrust the public school system. In some cases, schools in their neighborhoods are closed down without their input into the decision. These schools, in some cases, are hubs of the Black community. Furthermore, these parents do not trust or have a positive relationship with the schools because of their experiences when they were students. They were usually excessively disciplined and may not have their diploma.

Usually, they come to school ready to confront the teacher or the administration. They understand the unfairness in the system and want to advocate for their students, but on many occasions, due to lack of education, they do not understand how to champion on their child's behalf. Recently, a well-educated parent explained to me how her son's school did not want to follow his special education plan, which was mandated by the special education team at the school. She had to threaten to sue the district if he did not get what he deserved.

However, school districts depend on parents being naive of their rights. I have had to inform parents on several occasions to advocate in the best interest of their children. A few years ago, I had a student who served thirty-five days of in-school suspension. This was a blatant violation of his exclusive education rights. However, his parent did not have a clue. Why? Because public school failed her, and she was uneducated in the nuances of special education. A few years later, he was in a juvenile detention center. His story turned out to be tragic because a few weeks ago, he was killed in a shooting. I often think if a teacher or administrator had taken a real interest in him, he might be alive. He did not attend school much and was often suspended. This is only one example of how the white space in education can be deadly.

These are the situations parents often encounter in schools run by individuals who do not look like them or have their best interests at the forefront.

EDUCATION CAREERS FOUNDED ON SYSTEMIC RACISM

We cannot discuss the white space in public education without touching upon my experiences as a Black male educator. I possess four college degrees, but I have never really managed a school as the head principal. I have interviewed and been promised position, only to be passed over for whatever reason. I have one example in particular that proves this point.

CHARLES WHITE

In 2016, my school district called me to interview for a position as an assistant principal. I already had six years' experience as a building administrator. However, I was willing to remain in that job with the possibility of acquiring my own school in the future. The job was mine to turn down. Higher-ups told my then-boss to look for another teacher to fill my position at the juvenile detention center. I wanted to maintain my then-current level of income, so I asked the district to match my salary. I was immediately out of contention for the job after I made that request.

A colleague who was on the hiring committee informed me that I did not get the job because I was deemed too demanding. I, this Black man, was not worth a matching salary. The white guy hired for the job did not have the proper credentials and failed the principal test six times. He lasted a year and a half before he quit.

I felt worthless. My hard work meant absolutely nothing to my potential employers. No matter how hard a Black person works, we are still considered less qualified than a white guy with less education and experience. I tried for other jobs, but was never offered an interview. After that experience, I almost walked away from teaching, like countless other Black educators. However, I chose to remain because my students need me. I cannot be selfish and leave them.

CONCLUDING THOUGHTS

Until we address systemic racism, white supremacy, and implicit bias in the classroom, Black students will continue to suffer in segregated schools across the country. The suspension rates will continue to climb, and the school-to-prison pipeline will continue to send countless Black students into the dark hole of incarceration. I see countless highly intelligent children going to jail in some cases for decades. Why? Because the public school system failed to take an interest in them. Public schools should work in partnership with Black parents, not as adversaries. Too many educators give up on children of Color before seeing their true potential.

Every minute of my six years teaching in juvenile detention, there is a blessing to both my career and soul. When I first arrived in the classroom, there was no English curriculum. No textbooks, novels, writing materials, or grammar books. It was a wasteland. However, I didn't allow that to derail my vision. I acquired what I needed and began to teach. When the detention staff learned I was going to teach *Macbeth* to my students, they scoffed at the idea. They didn't believe that something as advanced as Shakespeare should be offered to my poor incarcerated students. Their doubt didn't stop me. I taught it, and my kids loved it. It was a success. I've had many more successes in the classroom, but that is one of my favorites.

It's one of my favorites because I exposed kids who are usually thrown away to an author many consider difficult to read and comprehend. However, at the end my students understood what was a soliloquy and dramatic irony. At first, they were afraid to read out loud and attempt to read the language but after much encouragement the classroom environment became relaxed. This was six years ago and the paraeducator who works with me still speaks of that lesson fondly. The lesson was a success not only because of what they learned. It was the relationship I built with those students that was invaluable.

CHARLES WHITE

I continue to teach in juvenile detention because to see a child grasp a poem, write a brilliant essay, or offer me a bit of wisdom is worth the few tough days I have. These children, at times, have no one to lean on. No parent is coming to visit. Some are abandoned to the system. I try to be the light they deserve. I attempt to bring a little happiness, love, and quality education to them. The relationships I've built with these students are invaluable. I can't see myself anywhere but there. I would be remiss if I did not also commend the white teachers on the frontlines teaching each child fairly. They advocate for all students regardless of race or background.

When I began teaching over twenty-four years ago, I made a promise to myself: To never forget the struggle of my ancestors so I could teach in our nation's schools. Years ago, I read W. E. B. Du Bois' book *The Souls of Black Folks*. It had significant impact on my life as a Black educator and human being. In the book, Du Bois speaks of "The Talented Tenth." The idea is that if you are fortunate enough to achieve an education, it's your duty as a member of that ten percent to bring others with you. It's your obligation to lift others up in the Black community.

This idea is the bedrock of what I do. This is why I attempt every day to dismantle the white supremist culture in our schools. I must tell the truth to my students and offer them the best education possible. If I don't, I am failing them. If I don't, I am not fulfilling the charge given to me by brother Du Bois over a hundred years ago. As stated in my first paragraph, slave masters didn't want an enslaved person to learn to read or to comprehend— because once you free a man or woman's mind, how can you expect them to remain a slave? Education is the key to deconstructing white spaces in America.

We must make all spaces in education fair to all children. We do not need white spaces; instead, let us transform them into human spaces.

Charles White is an educator with twenty-four years of experience. He teaches language arts to incarcerated students at a local juvenile detention center. He has been a writer for almost thirty years. He has won several poetry slams over the years, including one of six prizes in Westside Showroom's new play festival in 2018. He is a devoted husband of twenty years and the father of three children. He resides in Illinois.

SHAME 8
AS A PATH TO
HEALING RACISM

KIM McCAUL

S HAME HAS A BAD reputation. Being "crippled by shame"
sounds incredibly disempowering, and plenty of
coaches and generally well-meaning folk advise us not to
get stuck in shame, because "shame doesn't help anyone."
I used to operate from that space myself, seeing shame as
a pointless emotion to shift out of as quickly as possible.
But now I see that shame may have a really important role
to play as a catalyst for inner change. For white men like
me, when it comes to assuming responsibility for our role
in the systemic racism that defines our colonial societies,

really sinking into the truth of the situation and feeling the shame that will come with that can be just what we need to inspire us to take practical actions to undo racism and other systemic inequities.

It is not surprising to find that we white people are blind to racism. Our own cultural norms are hard to see. Every Western European born or descended person alive today grew up with a sense of normality around the fact that our people colonized (almost) every single country in the world. And most of us feel entitled to move across the world as we choose. To appreciate how racism is embedded in our psyche, we only need to see how difficult it is for us to realize that our entitlement of today is not "natural," but the result of a history in which our people subjugated and exploited everybody else.

Our ancestors did that, and we continue to benefit. If we were really to connect with this as a reality, shame and guilt would be natural responses. That we struggle so much to emotionally connect with this reality and feel our collective shame is, at least in part, a result of the fact that many of us have not dealt with our own personal shame and guilt. If we cannot hold the personal pain from our childhood, how can we hope to hold the vastness of the shame and guilt that is a natural human response to the mass murder, torture, rape, and exploitation that our ancestors visited upon People of Color across the planet?

Healing ourselves of racism involves healing ourselves of our individual trauma. Only then we can contribute to the healing of our collective trauma.

Shame and guilt are two deeply painful emotions that most of us carry from childhood. There are so many ways in which parents, teachers, or other significant adults induce shame and guilt in children. "That was a stupid thing to do," "God you are hopeless," "You make my life so hard," "Do you always have to be so difficult," "Stop being such a brat," "You are so annoying," "You should know the answer," et cetera. Phrases like that, other subtle shame-inducing behaviors like dismissiveness and neglect, and of course much worse and abusive ways of teaching a child there is something "wrong" with them, have sadly been part of many of our lives.

Psychologically, unprocessed shame and guilt can be experienced as actual threats to our identity, that is, our self-image as good and capable people. It is very natural to defend against such painful and challenging feelings by resisting anything that may induce them. But when it comes to healing traumas of the past, both individual and collective, it is important and healthy to be able to experience, process, and move through these emotions. When approached consciously they point us to the shadow parts of ourselves that we have pushed aside because we find them too painful or judge them as unacceptable. Thus, these emotions invite us to become more integrated human beings. This is a challenging journey. And unfortunately, men are still very much underrepresented when it comes to acknowledging, let alone actively pursuing healing of these wounds. As a result, unprocessed shame and guilt are a big reason so many of us have an instinctual resistance to acknowledging the existence of interpersonal and institutional racism and the benefits we (as white men) have gained as a consequence.

I first became aware of the link between our internalized

pain and shame, and our resistance to being open to the experiences of racism shared by People of Color, when watching *The Color of Fear*, a profound documentary on race relations in the United States. Produced by Chinese-American diversity educator Lee Mun Wah in 1994, sadly it has aged well; the intimate and heartfelt conversations it captures remain as relevant today as they were then. The documentary summarizes three days of conversations among a group of men—two African American, two Latino, two Asian American, and two white—as they grapple with questions such as how race impacts their life, why it is hard to talk about racism, and what it means to be American. What makes these conversations so powerful to witness and ensures their ongoing relevance, is that one of the two white men, David, says all the things white people unaware of their inherited racism say all the time: "I don't see your race," "Why can't we all just treat each other as human beings," "People of Color are always bringing up race, if they didn't there wouldn't be any of this struggle and strife," "Some of my dearest friends are People of Color," "Stop looking to the white man to fix your problems. Take responsibility for your own predicament." You may have heard statements like that from other white people and maybe you have uttered them yourself.

A group of highly articulate, passionate, and remarkably patient Men of Color confronts David and tackles each of his statements, again and again, despite the obvious emotional toll this takes on them. David deflects and rationalises away everything they say, no matter how heartfelt and deeply painful their personal sharing clearly is. Finally, after two and half days, his defenses crack.

Following an empathetic intervention by Lee Mun Wah, David starts to cry. Not in the deflecting way that some white people cry to escape a difficult conversation about racism and their own contribution, but in the way of a person who is actually contacting their own pain.

It emerges that David's inability to empathize with the other men has its origin in a deep inner disconnect from his own pain; essentially a lack of empathy for himself. In his case, much of the pain was caused by his own violent and explicitly racist father. In defending himself from the painful feelings of shame induced by his father, David had essentially cut himself off from his capacity to empathize with himself and others. This condition, a disconnect from our capacity to empathize, seems to be all too common among white men. I myself spent my youth in that state. I can also trace the cause for this to childhood factors and it manifested in quite extreme ways during my teenage years.

Unprocessed shame and guilt are a big reason so many of us have an instinctual resistance to acknowledging the existence of interpersonal and institutional racism and the benefits we (as white men) have gained as a consequence.

I grew up in Germany. My schooling was replete with learning about the Second World War, Germany's mass murder of millions of people, and the horrors of dictatorship. I resented it. Why should I feel guilty? In a classic contrarian move, I associated with Neo-Nazis. In fact, I probably would have qualified as a Neo-Nazi myself, even if I would never have admitted that. But I subscribed to a far-right newspaper and more than once raised my arm to a Hitler salute, even if only when drunk and "mucking around." I emotionally disconnected from what Nazi

KIM
McCAUL

Germany had actually meant. I said things like, "Well, Hitler did get the economy back on track," and found the idea of a strong leader kind of appealing because "at least they got things done." I was numb to the cost at which dictators get things done, the terrible impact they have on freedom, creativity, empathy, and compassion. I used racial slurs about people of Turkish and Arabic backgrounds (the most conspicuous minorities in Germany at the time). In those moments I did not experience them as equal human beings. I once participated in a fight with a group of Vietnamese-German kids and recall on another occasion watching a couple of skinheads I knew chase an African refugee through a park. I treated these incidents as entertainment and was totally disconnected from the effect they had on the people at the receiving end.

As I am writing these memories of my teenage years, shame and embarrassment re-surface. I can understand now why I was so disconnected. I carried a lot of pain and anger from the kind of everyday childhood traumas so many of us experience. The same kinds of traumas that make it so hard for many white people to accept that they have white privilege. Because they too had it hard. Today I can understand and empathize with the reasons why I was an emotionally disconnected, angry teenager and why I was attracted to a group that represented a big middle finger to social norms and expectations. At the same time, I am remorseful and ashamed for the way I expressed those unprocessed feelings. And I am glad that today I respond by feeling those feelings, because shame and remorse seem like appropriate emotions when seeing and acknowledging how my immaturity and disconnect caused pain to others.

After I finished high school, circumstances took me out of my small hometown and led me to spend time with open-minded people who, simply by their way of being, challenged my angry world view. As a result, I grew out of my extremist tendencies by my early twenties. But the unpacking of my own racism turned out to be a much longer, more intricate journey and confronting shame has been a recurring theme. Some years ago, I was in a training program in the U.S. to learn how to facilitate conversations about racism. I was the only white man in my cohort. During a break I chatted with an African American man who asked me what I was going to do with the training. I mused carelessly that I liked the idea of running workshops on racism but wasn't really sure how that would go, so I might not end up doing anything with it. Later that day the man I had spoken with raised our conversation in the group. He shared how hearing my casualness about what I'd do with this training really undermined his trust in me. He explained how for him racism was literally a matter of life and death and something he dealt with every single day. To have a white guy treat it as optional was very painful.

My initial reaction to this was to feel defensive, along the line of: "Well I have no idea how I will be able to invest my energy in this given it's not exactly a sought-after topic (certainly at that time in Australia it wasn't), and anyway it isn't my fault I am white and have the privilege to treat racism as optional." This was a classic case of what Robin DiAngelo has termed white fragility, a

KIM
McCAUL

spontaneous defensiveness in white people when confronted with their racial privilege. The man could have
swallowed his feelings. I am sure seeing a white guy treat
racism as optional was common to him. But by making
the emotional effort to speak up, he actually helped me
connect more deeply with my humanity and the reality
of racism. He made me see that, despite having spoken
about racism in occasional workshops for some years by
then, I was still keeping myself disconnected from the true
cost racism has on People of Color. And he helped me feel
in my body how the color of my skin gives me a choice
as to whether I deal with racism in my life or not. Waves
of shame and guilt arose naturally when I really allowed
that understanding to sink in, and that moment remains
a crucial reminder every time I become unconscious to
the impact of racism on People of Color and my privilege
to choose whether I challenge racism or not. Because as
a white man, it is only too easy to become unconscious
of racism again and again. And it turns out that as long
as I allow this unconsciousness to arise, a "luxury" I owe
entirely to my whiteness, there will be reasons to feel
ashamed. Here are some of the things that have caused
me to feel shame only recently:

1. An African American friend shared how she
   watched all four episodes of *When They See Us*
   in one sitting, and then allowed herself to fully
   experience the feelings of grief and pain for
   hours, owning them in her body. I felt shame
   at having stopped watching half-way through,
   because I could not stand witnessing the cruelty

and injustice suffered by the five boys, sentenced for a crime they did not commit. There I was sheltering myself from witnessing a pain my son is never likely to endure, while this Black woman was modeling owning the reality as the mother of a Black son.

2. Another African American friend shared how, since Ahmaud Arbery was murdered while jogging, she has been afraid to jog, fearing for her life every time she hears a car approach from behind. I felt shame for not having realized that this would be a likely impact for many African Americans, and from seeing that the fact that this did not even occur to me was a direct result of me being white as well as male.

3. At a Black Lives Matter rally, Aboriginal people shared about losing family in custody and regularly experiencing arbitrary police harassment. I felt shame at my sense of powerlessness and helplessness in the face of these systemic issues, as well as my ability to disconnect from that reality simply because of the color of my skin.

Versions of "I don't agree that I should feel guilty for my whiteness" are common in discussions about racism, even in contexts where nobody has mentioned anything about guilt. In fact, in most cases where I have seen that kind of statement used, there was no mention of guilt or shame until the white person brought up how they refuse to feel it. Which of course suggests that the feeling has already been triggered.

Instead of resisting that feeling, if you are white and especially a white man, I encourage you to open your heart to those feelings and appreciate their role in showing you areas for growth. By protecting yourself from your pain you are also cutting yourself off from the most precious expressions of your humanity. This is one of the big prices we white people are paying for the maintenance of racism. Disconnecting ourselves from our humanity, that is, our empathy, compassion, integrity, and capacity for healing.

There is no way you can justify your participation in a system of dominance over others, a system that is literally built on the exploitation of those who look different and on the theft of land and resources from Black and Brown people even to this day, without emotionally disconnecting. Feeling the shame and guilt for the actions of your ancestors or for your own past actions, inaction, ignorance, or disconnection is healthy. Not to wallow or indulge in endless self-flagellation. But to extend your emotional range and connect with your full humanity. Because behind the guilt and shame is your hurt and grief, and behind that your compassion, love, empathy, and your ability to contribute to the healing of our collective wounds.

Behind your guilt and shame is your true power.

Kim McCaul is of German and Irish descent and resides in Adelaide, Australia. He has spent the past twenty years working as an anthropologist on land rights and heritage matters with Aboriginal people across Australia. He is an author (*Multidimensional Evolution: Personal Expirations of Consciousness*), mediator, facilitator, and podcaster with a passion for reconciliation, universalism, cross-cultural bridge building, consciousness exploration, and our collective evolution.

MEETING FACE TO FACE 9

STEPHEN MATLOCK

R ECENTLY I WAS TALKING with a friend of mine in
another state. He's a Black pastor with a largely African American congregation, and he's worked diligently
for decades to build not just a people of faith but also a
safe and caring community. He and his friend, a white
pastor for a white congregation, have in the past brought
their churches together at special times of fellowship and
sharing. It's been a beautiful experience.

But my friend has run into some difficulties. We've all
seen the worldwide protests demanding we understand

that Black lives matter. This is something that is intuitive to Black folks, of course, and yet—it is strangely foreign to us white folks, who can assert *yes, Black lives matter*, but in the same breath say *no, we don't have to do anything to make it happen—it's really not that bad right now for our Black community, and besides, what really matters is something else entirely.*

This white pastor called on my friend to chat about these issues. That discussion became more of a listening session for my friend. His white friend decided to tell him what these issues really meant, and why there was a misunderstanding and even a contradiction between asserting the values of Black lives and what they both believed as Christians and pastors and men.

The conversation did not end with mutual understanding. What happened was just about the same as what often happens when white people try to talk with their Black friends: misunderstanding and confusion arise; battle lines are drawn; and both parties leave unsatisfied that nothing is accomplished.

This is not an unusual event. I have to tell you, in the space of a week, I've heard nearly this same story repeated by other friends, some who also serve in their faith communities, some who are just going about their business, sharing the discussions with their white peers about the issues of Black lives and how they matter. And almost always the chat concludes with both parties unsatisfied.

Why does this happen so frequently? None of these people could be considered "bad," in any sense of the word as we normally use it. These are good people, men and women, who say they seek understanding and want to bring healing. And yet—the conversations go south, nearly from the start.

THE DANGERS OF A LIMITED WORLDVIEW

We talked more, my friend and I. "Why can't my white friends hear me?" he asked.

I didn't hesitate in my answer. "Because when people hear something that contradicts who they know themselves to be, they feel threatened, are fearful of the change, and then do all they can to resist acknowledging the information so they can stay safe where they are. For white people, being asked to consider our elevated place in society is deeply disturbing—we can't acknowledge this obvious truth, and we can't accept any information that threatens our sense that it is right that we are so elevated, even as we will not admit to the elevation."

We both kinda laughed, and commiserated, and the conversation moved on to other things. But I thought about it later, not just the conversation itself, but also the catastrophic misunderstandings and broken connections that are the result.

Both of these pastors are good men. Both of them want to bridge the gaps. Both seek ways to do that. But the conversations—and the multiple conversations just like it—fail to achieve that goal.

The problem is not the willingness for people to have conversations. It's not unequal levels of education—both men are trained with similar theological education at similar divinity schools that grant similar degrees.

It's something much simpler, and yet profound: both of

STEPHEN
MATLOCK

these men start from different beginnings. Their world-views differ, and because these differences are not mutually acknowledged, the real conversations fail. My friend, the Black pastor, will always start from his place as a Black man in America. There is no way to get around this essential fact. He must consider this when he sends his child off to school, when he drives to his business office, when he takes his wife out for dinner, when he considers his opportunities to speak in front of other groups.

His friend, the white pastor, will always start from his place as a man who happens to be white, but who, like many white men, sees himself as the "neutral, objective observer." Unlike my friend who is reminded daily that he is Black by the world around him, his friend exists in a world that seldom overtly reminds him of his elevated position in society. It is just normal. It is normal to send your kids to school and think nothing more about them and their safety until they return. Normal to drive anywhere you want and be untroubled by the police. Normal to show up at any restaurant and get a table with no hassle. Normal to be invited to speak and teach to any group with a budget for speaking fees. Normal, even, to have a discussion with a Black friend without acknowledging their Blackness.

We can agree that this is a sad situation full of misunderstanding—but I want to point this out: what results from not acknowledging race is that white people might not be able to connect at a meaningful level with their friends who are not white.

Your first reaction might be this: "But *I'm* different. I don't see color. I love all my friends equally." Perhaps you do. But I want to be clear in what I say: Despite your pro-testations of "love" and meaning well, your beliefs about yourself and your friends are inaccurate. And because your beliefs are inaccurate, you limit the quality of the connections that you are having with those people whom you call your friends. You cannot have a true, honest, mutual connection with someone when you refuse to see them—*all* of them, even the parts that go against how you think they should be.

I do not say any of this lightly. White people have been blinded, deliberately, into thinking that being white is not a significant thing about ourselves. That blindness leads to our failure to see how our whiteness can negatively impact the people whom we claim to "love" and "respect." Until we get our vision checked, we will never see our disconnected state.

We are going to always be in the position of never having a fully open, direct connection with our friends who are not white. The racial dynamics of American life today inhibit honest communication. We might not think this is true while we're having drinks with our friends who assure us we're "not like the other white people." But in reality, we are like other white people, and it's a socially convenient and safe thing to respond like that, especially after we directly question our friends about the intimacy of our friendship.

We need to consider that we can complicate the lives of our friends just by our reactions, whether we are aware of them or not. We can interfere with their jobs, their education, and their families. If we call the police, we are more likely to be believed than they will. If we start a fight with them, they are more likely to be blamed. It's better that they lie to us to keep the peace than rouse us in anger with truth. I've been there when those assertions of friendship are raised; I've watched this happen; and I've listened to the conversations later. Unacknowledged whiteness kills connections.

HOW WE GET OUT OF THIS MESS

MEETING
FACE TO FACE

If you're like me, a white person in America, you were raised to believe that you are just an American. The average Joe or Jane. Your school, family, church, government, entertainment, business career, even graveyards are likely to be overwhelmingly white. And you can't imagine that life is any different for anyone else in America. "Pull yourself up by your bootstraps!" "Reach for the stars!" "Hard work is the only way to success!" "Laziness will always destroy you!" I'm sure you've heard these lessons, and maybe more.

But these aphorisms are simply not true for the rest of Americans who are not born and raised white. The most salient fact that distinguishes different experiences in America is not our income or education or parents or even politics. Unfortunately, our *race* determines our *place*—and the benefits that flow to white people, that are throttled for other Americans, depend upon this one fact.

This is not an attempt to make you feel guilty or to push you into shame. I'm just saying this system is wrong. And without a sense of wanting to change this, at the deepest level, we will never be able to make this right. The way to get out of this mess of frozen hierarchies and mistaken beliefs is to be open to the reality of the world around us, unfiltered by our viewpoints that put us smack dab in the center of things as "neutral" or even beneficent observers. We have got to get a better understanding of ourselves as people who are white. We have got to grasp the truth that not only does it matter that our Black friends are Black—it matters to us that we've often let whiteness isolate us, leading us to say and do things that have damaged the lives of Black people.

What I'm asking us to do is to acknowledge that we've been lied to about our own selves, and about those around us. We've been snookered into believing that there's a material difference in our fellow humans that's based upon their appearance, and we've let that lie turn us away from others. So it's time to acknowledge that training, that it happened, that's it's keeping us from human intimacy, and that it is not only possible to see our friends for their Blackness, but to enjoy them for all they are in their Blackness. What we have offered to us by leaving behind our fears and our doubts is the joy of authentic, open friendships, of hearing our friends, sharing in their dreams, being with them in their pain, living with them in their lives.

THE BENEFITS OF CHANGE

Getting to honesty with ourselves and about ourselves has many benefits. We don't have to maintain so many lies about ourselves, our motives, and our actions. We don't

STEPHEN
MATLOCK

have to worry about our place in life being usurped by another and then spend so much of our energy furiously attempting to continue in our denials that justice was done when someone better was advanced. We learn the value of speaking our minds, honestly and directly. We can talk about contentious issues as if they are important—and they often are!—but without the hard shell of our identity keeping us from admitting fault or seeing reason. (I suspect the key reason that there was such a disconnect in the conversation between my friend and his white friend was due more to the fear of stepping out of place as a white pastor leading a white church. Imagine the consequences of not toeing the line as a white leader. How constraining that restriction can be!)

The thing I want to emphasize, however, is the benefit of simply *seeing* people. You can see your friend as Black. Or Asian. Or gay. Or Muslim. Or trans. Or whomever they are in the moment: a glorious, unique individual who never existed before and never will again, a gift to you in this life to experience and enjoy and love. You don't have to pretend that you do not *see* the obvious, and you do not have to pretend that it doesn't *matter*. Your friends know who they are—imagine how much they will see your respect and love for them when you acknowledge them—when you *include* them—for who they are: no more, no less, but fully human and lovable and embraceable. It *matters* that your friend is Black. It *matters* that your friend is gay. It *matters* that your friend is Muslim. That is a valuable part of their identity. They don't deny it. Why not see them the way that they are, and tear down the barriers?

White people can get stuck in a place where we are locked in whiteness. Perhaps we are tempted to try this—this freedom to see people as they are, learn to celebrate diversity, to call in, not shut out, to enjoy the wonderful differences. How do we get from here to there?

The key is *relationships*. First and last and only. It's the hardest thing possible, I know. And I can hear you right now asking "How can you tell me to have relationships when you've just got done telling me that I don't have *any* relationships?"

That's the question I wanted you to ask! Because now you are ready for the steps. You are where you are because you are not seeing, or listening, or feeling, or enjoying. So the ways out are going to involve all of these, and they are going to involve you and the things that you do, as well as the people that you *will* meet in your journey.

Most of us have the internet at our fingertips twenty-four hours a day. So use your technological freedom to explore what people are saying, most especially people who are not like you and people who have contradictory beliefs to you. Challenge yourself here to read and listen. Go read up on Black Lives Matter, for example. Read *their* website, watch *their* videos, listen to *their* speakers. If you spend your time listening only to those who already see things your way, who explain Black lives to you and define Black values to you—you are learning second-hand. Go learn for yourself!

STEP ONE: Read books and articles and magazines, listen to music, watch videos, attend exhibits and plays and dances and protests created by those who are outside your current sphere of consumption, works created by Black, Indigenous, and People of Color (BIPOC), to help you to *see* people, to *listen* to what they say, and to *understand* who they are. You will not be able to connect with people who are not just like you if you make no attempt to first understand them. (Hint: people are individuals. If you learn this in your work, you've already learned the primary lesson.)

You've got an education now, and you're listening to Black opinions? Great. Time for—

STEP TWO: Get to know people individually, and get to know their values and strengths. This is going to take more than just reading and listening and thinking. At this point, it's time for you to move. You shop, right? You get supplies, right? You have business meetings, right? You have Facebook and Twitter and Instagram and Snapchat. So start making friends, even if they're really just acquaintances—for now.

Follow Black people on social media. Try buying your goods and supplies from Black businesses. Seek out Black peers in your business. Spend as much time as possible simply listening to them. You don't need to give your opinion. You're likely not ready to even ask questions. Just listen and learn. See if you can understand without asking questions because you're listening and attempting to understand the context of the discussions. If listening raises questions, answer your questions with your own research and learning, and use resources by Black people and from Black organizations.

If you're a religious believer, seek out fellow believers

116

in Black religious organizations—for listening, *not* for telling. Nothing about your faith demands that you avoid listening to others, so use your opportunities to listen to a diverse set of people and beliefs. You'll learn a lot about your own faith and what it means because you're examining it.

Proceed at your own speed, but do this with diligence because you want to know people. Do a lot of listening, and then, as you find yourself able to, offer support to Black-led organizations with your donations. Yes, pay for the education and uplift that you receive. You probably understand the tradition of offering support when you receive from another.

STEPHEN
MATLOCK

And along the way of learning and seeing and listening and understanding . . . you will start making friends. Because you have been learning how to see people and how to love them *as they are and without precondition*, you are going to find like-minded people who are on the journey with you, and you will also find people who will let you into their lives because you are loving, kind, gentle, and careful to see them as they are.

You will start finding the intimacy of friendships you lacked when you stayed in your whiteness. I guarantee this. It may be quite a long time—you have a lifetime of wrong behaviors and wrong attitudes to unlearn!—and at times it will be frustrating. You will make *many* mistakes. I guarantee that, as well.

But what you will find are not simply parallel friendships that are similar to what you have right now. You will find that you are enjoying a wider diversity of people, some with absolutely contrary opinions and ideas to yours, some who will seem like long-lost family, some who will be your ally, and some who will treat you with honesty that leaves you breathless.

You will discover the most enjoyable thing about life itself: you will discover living. You will discover the wonderful joy of meeting face-to-face with those whom you love even as you acknowledge they are wonderfully different. And there is nothing in this world worth more than that.

You will have taken many risks to step out of whiteness, but there will be so much reward for taking them. I urge you to take the first step: Start to listen.

Stephen Matlock is a part-time author and gardener in the Pacific Northwest, often overwhelmed by both words and weeds. He has been writing about his journey into inclusion and diversity for a dozen years. His most recent short story, "To Sleep, Perchance to Dream," was published in *Literally Stories*.

PART III

PREPARING YOURSELF
TO BE AN ALLY

AWARENESS AND EDUCATION: CREATING A BEAUTIFUL FUTURE

10

CONSUELO G. FLORES

O N SEPTEMBER 20, 2019, my heart blew up. I felt like the Grinch when he finally understood what love is and his "small heart grew three sizes that day." I had known beautiful love before, but not like what I felt when I met my grandson Benjamin, minutes after his birth. I've never felt that kind of instant, enormous, and profound love. My son is Mexican American and my daughter-in-law is Black, making Benjamin, my precious grandson, biracial.

Eight months after Benjamin was born, America experienced a racial awakening. In the spring of 2020, after police killed yet another Black man, George Floyd, protest marches quickly filled the streets in hundreds of cities across the United States. Within days the campaigns for police reform and anti-racism grew into an international phenomenon as multitudes of people throughout the world turned out to support Black families, friends, colleagues, and more often than not, strangers.

George Floyd's murder angered and saddened many and moved us into action, to not only show solidarity by marching, but also by seeking to learn more about the Black experience. In countless businesses and organizations, new initiatives were launched, new policies were put in place, new inclusion efforts made, and difficult conversations on race, unearned white privilege, and inequity started. This collective awakening of what it's like to be Black while living in America resulted in non-Black people by the thousands finally starting to listen to their Black fellow citizens.

In my place of employment, staff decided to hold community chats to facilitate understanding and offer support to those who'd joined the protests. It was during one of these discussions that a biracial colleague shared what she'd experienced. After joining a protest near her home, a Nazi militia member confronted her, pulling a gun and threatening to kill her.

She didn't leave home for weeks after that.

It's not like she could change clothes and confuse her attacker. It's not like she could dye her hair and make herself different so her attacker wouldn't recognize her. It's

AWARENESS
AND
EDUCATION:
CREATING
A BEAUTIFUL
FUTURE

not like she could change her lifestyle and suddenly be acceptable to her attacker. It's not like she could grow a new skin that would not be Black.

I am not Black and I will never pretend to know what it's like to live with Black skin. I do have an idea based on my personal experiences as a Latina in which I've faced discrimination, profiling, and outright attacks as well. BUT, even so, having an idea and actually living the often more severe experiences Black people face are two very different realities. Thus, I have taken it upon myself to learn as much as I can by reading and talking with my Black friends and colleagues about their experiences—their hard truths, even and particularly now.

CONSUELO
G. FLORES

Hard truths about race are not easy to process, especially if we already feel guilty for either not experiencing them ourselves, not paying attention to them when they happen in front of us, or worse yet seeing them and doing nothing.

My colleague cried as she talked about the effect her attacker's threat had on her and her family. What drove home the heinous reality of anti-Black racism was my darker-skinned colleague's declaration, her voice shaking and hands trembling: "And she's a light-skinned Black woman."

My colleague's statement was not lost on me. Even though my grandson is a light-skinned Black boy, he'll face the same myriad of challenges that my colleagues face. He has a higher chance of becoming a statistic than a success. And I can't, won't, allow that to happen. I may not be Black, but that hasn't stopped me from learning about the Black experience.

AWARENESS
AND
EDUCATION:
CREATING
A BEAUTIFUL
FUTURE

I have always learned from and about the diverse people I've interacted with, by focusing a large part of my formative years reading books about other cultures, other ethnicities, other histories. As a child, I wanted to be like Harriet Tubman, speak like Frederick Douglass, and make scientific discoveries like George Washington Carver. I had a better understanding of the world around me as well as drew inspiration from these icons of American history with whom I could identify. Their life stories and their commitment to making the lives of those around them better, resonated with me.

For my sophomore and junior years in high school, I attended an all-girls' Catholic school and it was the first time I clearly understood discrimination. In that school, I had few friends and all—with one lone exception—were girls of Color. We didn't fit in with the majority of the white girls and sought out each others' company during the dreaded recess and lunch breaks. Still, my experiences with being "othered" were not as intense as those of my Black friends.

I didn't understand why we were shunned. I didn't understand why my friend's skin color decided her fate. I would think to myself, that if the white girls would only talk with us, they'd know that we were fun, nice, and smart. We could even become friends. I also didn't know why even the administrators seemed to subscribe to shunning us or questioning our abilities, especially given that we had to be accepted into the school to begin with. And despite my knowing about and reading great Black writers on my own, the books we were assigned to read in this school were almost entirely written by old, white men.

It wasn't until my senior year, when I transferred into a more progressive high school, that my homework assignments, as well as the student body, truly reflected the diverse world I had learned about in my childhood and come to appreciate so highly.

During my last year of high school, I lived in a dormitory on campus. I lived with people from all over the United States and all over the world—Georgia, New York, California, Afghanistan, Japan, Egypt, Mexico, and Iran. I learned more about diversity and differences between cultures than I ever had before. I also learned how similar "different" people are.

CONSUELO
G. FLORES

At this second high school, I learned that love of family is the same no matter where you come from. I learned that people from any group can be hurtful, and people from any group can love you, hold you up, and inspire you. During my senior year of high school, I became part of a larger family, a larger human family, and I understood how we were all different yet still connected. As a family we were all (and should still be) accountable to each other, learn about each other, care about each other.

As I became an adult, the experiences of my youth shaped my perspective and my understanding that to make the world a better place, I must learn not only from books and sciences, but also from and about each other through life experiences. My life's focus and passion was to educate myself about other people's experiences—knowing that one person's truth could not possibly represent everyone from their specific background. And so my personal quest to be inclusive, have diverse friends, create space for differences within my life, and instill in my own family the value of acceptance, became not only my mantra but my professional focus as well.

Though I'd read many books written by Black authors and had intentionally created an inclusive, intimate circle of friends from all backgrounds, it wasn't until I worked professionally in promoting diversity that I truly understood the specific challenges of the Black community. Within my career I witnessed the insidiousness of racism cushioned in the most seemingly benign manner. This job gave me an additional perspective of the Black experience, this time in a corporate environment.

AWARENESS
AND
EDUCATION:
CREATING
A BEAUTIFUL
FUTURE

The Black experience, the Black narrative, attacks on the Black body, are a bit different—sometimes more subtle—in corporate America than they are on the street, yet these realities are just as important for us to dismantle to create a more level, equitable, and fair playing field. Within the context of corporate America, Black people encounter racism before they walk in the door. On resumes, their names are met with negative bias before they are hired, and candidates are labeled as the "diversity" hire after landing the job. Oftentimes, when layoffs occur, Black employees are first to go, a frequent occurrence during challenging economic times. And in the larger world of industry relations, executives at the highest levels are predominantly white men, demonstrating by example that corporate America is still a white boys club. A level playing field would not allow for this to be the case. It would mean more equitable opportunities within the business sector, industry, and media that reflect the world of inclusion I've come to appreciate. It would mean we all had a fair chance of being seated at the table.

But that understanding and representation means commitment, work, and getting out of the comfort zone of familiarity. For me to change—to truly embrace change—I knew I needed to start from a place of knowing that I was ignorant of the Black experience. It was important for me to learn and reflect on the stories coming from the Black community. This meant not only listening to those in my community who face the greatest risk of being directly hurt by racist actions; I must also speak out the moment I see things happening to my fellow Black Americans, especially because I am not Black. I want that for my Black grandson.

CONSUELO
G. FLORES

I admit that I do see color. Saying I don't see color would negate the experiences of my Black colleagues. Like we are doing at work, I now talk about race with my family and friends when the opportunity arises, understanding how the history of racism, othering, persecution, and destruction is still reflected in how our society functions today.

I remember when I was looking for a new home to rent some years ago, I was moving from a mostly white neighborhood that was viewed as "upscale," "nice," and "with good schools." I eventually found a beautiful, more affordable home in an "urban" area of Los Angeles where the community was mostly Black. When I let friends know that I was moving into this neighborhood, I was immediately met with concerns for my safety.

I decided to do a little research, as I always do, and discovered that my former "nice" neighborhood had more assaults, rapes, and even murders listed in the online public reports on crime than my new "urban" neighborhood.

I've happily and comfortably lived in my beautiful, more affordable home for more than six years. I don't act on things based on hearsay. I research and investigate a situation myself to make my own informed decisions.

When I talk with family, learn about friends, or discover things about them or myself that I may not like, I see it as an opportunity for growth. I know I must be willing to be uncomfortable when facing hard truths regarding racism or even microaggressions—whether they exist within me or my inner circle. It's not an easy conversation to have with family and it's even harder with friends, especially if I value the friendship but don't like the behavior.

An example of a microaggression presented itself to me during the pandemic shutdown of 2020. A (white) friend of mine posted an article on his social media page about how the European Union had formally blocked Americans from entering their countries due to the spike in COVID-19 infection rates in the United States. A comment left by one of his white friends questioned whether the "riots, arson, destruction of property, extreme violence, and lawlessness going on here (the U.S.) affected their decision as well. That kind of virus can spread just as quickly as COVID-19 and potentially have even more damage in the long run," he concluded.

I thought about this white man's comment and realized that his focus was not about the protests to stop the killing of Black people by police but on the destruction of property and the limitation or inconvenience of not being able to travel to Europe. I felt compelled to respond and so I commented that I "wouldn't doubt it if all the police brutality, violence against peaceful protests, and flagrant

AWARENESS
AND
EDUCATION:
CREATING
A BEAUTIFUL
FUTURE

racism going on here affected their decision as well. That kind of virus can spread just as quickly as COVID-19 and potentially have even more damage in the long run—just ask the descendants of the slaves brought over from Africa or the families of Eric Garner, Philando Castile, or George Floyd, just to name three."

I would not have been able to respond to this comment and address his complete lack of understanding and focus, had I not been committed to educating myself about the Black experience, being an active listener to my Black friends and colleagues, and bringing all of that knowledge to my answer.

The spring of 2020 was a zeitgeist moment, ripe with opportunities to truly learn about each other and ourselves. I acknowledge that this collective awakening of what it's like to be Black while living will always be part of the American fabric in all of our lives because of this moment. However, to make this a lasting change in my life, I commit to continue doing my part in moving our country forward from this flashpoint in our history. I commit to doing right by Benjamin.

Everyone should have a Benjamin in their lives. Someone who represents hope, who is unstained, who instantly holds hearts that grow three times their size, simply because this Benjamin exists. A Benjamin, like my grandson, can provide even the most unenlightened or hardened of people the chance of unencumbered, unpolluted, pure love. The crux is being open to that possibility, being open to a literal change of heart.

But change is hard. Real change, in which Black Americans are accepted, loved for who they are, fully supported,

CONSUELO
G. FLORES

encouraged, and given equal opportunities to succeed, is harder but important and necessary. I know that if I'm truly committed to this most essential change for my Black sisters and brothers—for my grandson—to be truly real, to take root, to grow into a way of loving and living and not be for just a moment, I must take personal responsibility to research, read, and create an understanding approach and then pass it on to those around me. I must be willing to listen and grow even if it's uncomfortable. I must continue building outward from my insular inner circle.

AWARENESS
AND
EDUCATION:
CREATING
A BEAUTIFUL
FUTURE

I take great personal pleasure in knowing that because of my commitment to learning about diversity from a young age, I passed that onto my now adult sons. Their friends throughout their lives were from all ethnic backgrounds. I loved watching them play with friends as children, then date as teens, and finally marry partners who are Chinese American and Black American. I love that my family is inclusive and that my first grandchild is biracial. I owe him a future that is inclusive and supportive of all he is. That is my promise to Benjamin.

I love my family. It's an amazing microcosm of the possibility of what our country can be.

And it is truly beautiful.

The youngest of ten siblings in a Mexican immigrant family, multidisciplinary artist *Consuelo G. Flores* is a Legacy Artist of the world-renowned Self Help Graphics & Art in East Los Angeles, honored for her decades of cultural work. She's Director of Policy, Strategy & Analysis in the Equity & Inclusion Department at SAG-AFTRA, promoting diversity in the entertainment industry since 2000.

WHAT NOT TO SAY 11

SYLVIA WOHLFARTH

I AM HALF NIGERIAN and half Irish living in Ireland. So
when I sat down to begin writing this chapter, curious
as I am, I wanted to understand why systemic racism is
still rampant in the United States and looked closer at
the Jim Crow Laws of the southern states which, until the
sixties, were in place for almost one hundred years. I was,
to say the least, horrified at the inhumanness of such a
pervasive system. Fortunately, over the past sixty years or
so, there has been a decline in overt and institutional racism, but at the same time, many white people still covertly

have negative associations with and feelings toward Black people—"feelings they largely don't acknowledge because they conflict with their ideas about themselves being egalitarian," according to Professor Thomas E. Ford in "Psychology behind the unfunny consequences of jokes that denigrate."

I knew then that to start writing I had to feel the pain personally and not vicariously. I decided to go back to my childhood and filter out lived moments of racial discrimination to personalize my story. This, I felt, would help me to better understand how racism affects one's soul, as well as justify my writing this essay.

I was born in Nigeria, a country where skin colour was not necessarily a symbol for acceptance—other socio-cultural indicators assigned you your rightful place in society. My father was a Nigerian doctor and my mother an Irish accountant. I experienced the first nine years of my life within a system of being regarded as either Nigerian and Black (with its complex number of ethnic groups), half Nigerian and Brown (me), white, or miscellaneous non-Black (Lebanese, Cypriots, and Indians, etc.). As a family, we were privileged.

At the age of nine, I was sent to boarding school in Ireland. And it was during my holiday stays with my grandmother there that I had my first encounters with discrimination. There were not many Black people in Ireland during the sixties and early seventies so I was a bit of an exception. And yes, my hair, my curly hair. How mortified I would feel at being asked by strangers if they could touch my hair: "It looks so soft," they'd say. A question that wasn't a question and I would let them stroke my head and listen to them drool over my hair—as soft as the sacrificial lamb's wool.

Living now in Ireland after over forty years in Germany, I do volunteer work with a group of young Black African girls (many second-generation kids) and racism is often a topic. They, too, could relate to my hair story. "Can I feel your hair?" "Is it real?"

Does it matter? Would you like it if someone asked if they could touch your hair and if it were real? This is rude.

What really hurt me the most though and shaped my personality were the times walking through mostly working-class estates when children would stop playing and shout 'blacky' at me. Children can be cruel if not taught to be respectful of others, and their antennas pick up every derogatory remark made by adults. Even to this day, I take a deep breath before opening the door and walking into a group of strangers. Aware that I might be trespassing on white spaces. But this is my adult problem, my lack of self-confidence, expecting the worst, the quizzical look.

Then came my teenage years and early puberty and my encounters with boys, and, uncomfortably too, men. If this was not told to me directly, then I'd often hear from a friend that so-and-so thinks you're very sexy, you look so exotic and racy. I'd blush with mortification and make sure my clothing was always more than appropriate.

These experiences of endured and suppressed hurts are manifested in my lack of self-confidence. My hair reminded me I was different, I avoided walking through areas where children were playing, and one of the first questions I asked my first boyfriend was whether he thought I looked like a prostitute.

SYLVIA
WOHLFARTH

This chapter is only an introductory step to clearing the stony path towards racial equality and inclusivity. Learning "what not to say" to avoid hurt and embarrassment is learning to tread carefully on a history of pain while we heal on our way to bridging the divide.

DON'T SAY THIS TO PEOPLE OF COLOR

The current societal upheaval following the brutal murders of Black Americans by police officers has led to a surge in widespread protests and national and worldwide support for the Black Lives Matter movement. Awareness of what is happening has penetrated through the backyards and into the living rooms of both Black and white Americans. I note a palette of intergenerational feelings and emotions—a collective melting pot mixed with anger, horror, pain, embarrassment, non-acceptance, justification, and even hate.

Within this moment of shock, uncertainty, and self-doubt regarding one's own inherent racism, self-reflection, and reflection in general, one thing is clear: Things cannot remain the way they are and, in the name of humanity, change has to happen. Decades of the self-protective 'talk' with one's Black children were the norm and now the time has come when the focus must be on bringing people of all races together to talk to each other and build relationships of understanding and trust. We owe this to our children.

What we must realize as well is that racism is the heritage of white America, and white Americans have to learn how to deal with it and take ownership of this history.

Black Americans have the stories and the experience of living in the midst of abject racism and so now, it's their right to be listened to. Only then can we jointly bring about any sustainable change. Owning and accepting racism as a white-induced socio-political system is the first step towards healing and achieving an inclusive society.

Dialogue has never been as imperative as it is today, and it is not only the United States which is experiencing a deep division politically and socio-culturally—this is happening worldwide.

Black people are no longer willing to put up with white discriminatory language or watch their culture being misappropriated. A typical example of: We love and want your music and athleticism, but we don't need you. The latter happens when a dominant culture (white) inappropriately takes, for their own financial gain, aspects from another culture that is experiencing oppression (Black minority culture) with no understanding or acknowledgement of its origins or significance.

SYLVIA
WOHLFARTH

Taking the example of music, while it is not exclusive to one person or one group, it becomes problematic when there is a lack of understanding between the connection of the genre and its history, Rachel Bresnahan explains in "Appropriation vs. Appreciation in Music: Where Should We Draw the Line?"

Genres like the blues, jazz, hip-hop, and rap have their roots in the struggles of racial oppression. Because white musicians cannot establish the emotional connections based on themes like racial oppression, they strip the music of its quintessential contexts.

By failing to give people credit for their own culture,

cultural misappropriation reinforces the power imbalance between the dominant and minority groups.

White Americans are facing accusations of historic and systemic racism pervasive in society, and rightly so. While, additionally, many Black Americans feel their white counterparts don't know or understand them, or even try.

It is all the more important to not simply support Black people in regaining their pride and to demonstrate against structural racism. Now is the time to talk to each other with respect and acknowledgement.

RESPECTFUL COMMUNICATION

Racist comments come in all forms and intensity, whether intentional (downright racial abuse) or unintentional in the form of varying insensitive levels of micro-aggressive behavior. (See the following chapter.)

Learning "what not to say" is not a stand-alone. Understanding how racism works and how to dismantle it is the underlying message of any dialogue between people of different colour: A two-way interaction based on respect for the other.

As white Americans in conversation with fellow Black Americans, it is crucial to bear in mind that within the whole issue of racism and the centuries-old suffering of Black Americans, you are treading on the path of their pain. It is not your suffering, so you shouldn't throw in words of hopelessness and self-pity.

"Oh, I never realized just how terrible it was ... I feel so bad ... you poor people ... what can I do (for me)?" Compassion can be noted and acknowledged. Leave it at that.

140

If the subject of racism comes up in a conversation, then listen. Understand that when a Person of Colour talks to you about racism, it's their story they are telling. They are trusting you. Treat that trust with the utmost respect. It's not a question of personal blame or justification but one of responsibility.

If a Person of Colour tells you they've been racially discriminated against, don't go on the defensive or look for explanations or excuses. You can't imagine the pain if you haven't experienced it yourself. Don't judge or disrespect their experience with explanations like:

"Are you sure that's what they meant?" Or "Don't you think you're being a bit too sensitive?"

And don't make light of what is said with reactions like: "Look, things aren't as bad as they used to be . . . I'm sure we'll get over this soon . . . it's only a matter of time."

People of Colour are suffering racial discrimination today. Do not silence or stifle the voices of People of Colour. They need to speak up; their voices need to be heard and understood in order to initiate change.

Don't bring up the subject of racism just because you are talking to a Black person. Discuss things as you would with your white counterparts unless your partner specifically wishes to talk about racism. And then listen.

If you have a racial consciousness, don't be self-righteous about it. Don't boast. Statements like "I'm not racist, I've some Black friends" or "I don't notice colour" are counterproductive. Seeing colour is ingrained. I can myself recall going up to the top of a London bus and being struck by how few, if any at all, white people were to be seen although the bus was full.

SYLVIA
WOHLFARTH

141

Never presume that when you see a Black person in a space usually taken up by white people that they don't belong there. Don't ask the person to explain and justify their presence. I remember being at a party of a good friend of mine in Germany and being the only Person of Colour present. I knew most of the other guests but not my friend's family members. I happened to be sitting next to my friend's brother who I noticed was trying to think of something to say, when suddenly he blurted out "Are you my sister's cleaning lady?" He had been desperately trying to figure why someone like me, who he'd never seen before, was at this party. He knew his sister had a South American woman who regularly cleaned the house so I guess this is how he defined my role and presence. It was quite embarrassing for all concerned.

It is, in fact, wiser to say nothing at all than to say something that might be considered discriminatory and hurtful. This shows you are aware and have the right amount of sensitivity.

Saying "I didn't mean to say that" makes it even worse "Don't take it so seriously, it was only a joke."

Things said as a joke or in pity cannot be retracted once you notice you have caused someone pain or embarrassment.

Any attempt to amuse through the denigration of a social group or its representatives is what is called disparagement humor, Professor Ford says.

These are sexist or racist jokes—basically, anything that makes a punchline out of a marginalized group, "disguising expressions of prejudice in a cloak of fun."

Another extremely sensitive area is ethnic/racial teasing

among peers. This is often a common form of adolescent interaction centering around race and is "a unique form of discrimination characterized by humor," according to Sara Douglass et al. in "'They Were Just Making Jokes': Ethnic/Racial Teasing and Discrimination Among Adolescents." So as not to seem uncool, young people who are the targets of ethnic/racial teasing often tend to pretend that what was said is funny and hide their hurt.

"Just because you don't say you don't like us doesn't mean we don't see it."

People who have suffered racism are extremely sensitive, often insecure, and sometimes angry. Their antennas are attuned to how something is said and its effect. They can discern genuine concern.

SYLVIA WOHLFARTH

In interpersonal dialogue, body language plays a huge role. So, you don't need to put on an artificial smile or go out of your way to be extra nice because a person is Black and you want to show your political correctness. It looks so condescending. Just be friendly, supportive, and inclusive.

PHRASES YOU SHOULDN'T SAY
IN YOUR PERSONAL AND PROFESSIONAL LIFE

I'd like to mention some examples of daily micro-aggressive "no-nos" that second-generation People of Colour in countries like Britain or Germany experience:

"Where did you learn your English/German? It's almost perfect."

"Where do you come from? No, I mean where do you really come from?"

143

"Do you know what I mean?" Black Africans in particular dislike this question as they feel it implies they are stupid. If you are genuinely interested in a Person of Colour's opinions, ask them straight out. Don't ask their white friend: "Does she/he like living in Germany/Britain?" (This is typical for the older generation.)

Or imagine being told to your face by a family member: "I don't like Black people/foreigners, there are too many here." Or "I always wait until I get a German taxi driver. I don't want to have to get into a taxi with a foreigner."

This, for me, is colourism. Whereby, because I'm light-coloured and speak 'proper' English, I'm allowed to belong, and be considered 'white' enough to understand one's dislike of 'foreigners.'

As a professional—medical staff, lawyer, teacher, police officer, boss, colleague, or service recipient—listen to and mirror the person with whom you're speaking. Basic politeness is requisite for an inclusive society. We were all born with antennas, admittedly some better attuned than others, so make sure you show respect equally.

The following are some examples of real-life situations where I'd like you to reflect on how you would feel if you were the recipient of the questions and statements:

A doctor says to a Black patient who is complaining about severe attacks of colic: "Are you sure the pain is as bad as you say it is? I've heard that people from Africa, especially women, have a lower pain threshold and even tend to moan out loud? It's their culture, I'm told!"

A teacher says to one of her Black students: "Today, we're going to talk about Trans-Atlantic slavery. Can you tell the class something about this topic? I know your parents come from Nigeria in West Africa where the slave trade began." All heads turn to listen to the very embarrassed student who doesn't know any more about the subject than the rest of her classmates.

A police officer interviews a Black woman who is reporting her distressful confrontation with an exhibitionist. "Has this happened to you before and how often? You know there is a tendency for women of Colour and from other cultures to find themselves in the role of victims."

A boss asks one of his Black employees, "Would you mind attending our next international meeting? We need to show how diverse our company is."

A college student tells her Black friend: "Don't take this personally but when I have children, I want them to grow up in a white environment as I did."

Some of these examples of what one shouldn't say to Black people are said without reflection, while some are downright racist. By the latter I mean discriminatory or derogatory statements made, as in the above examples, by the police officer and doctor. These are instances of racial stereotyping statements based on assumptions deriving from perceptions about race or skin colour, more brutal in their effect as they are made by people in power. Statements that would never be made to white people.

• • •

I'd like to finish my essay with another little personal story of an experience I had regarding colour and inclusiveness.

After having lived for over forty years in Germany, I moved back to Ireland three years ago. Arriving in my car at Immigrations, I handed my Irish passport to the officer wondering how he would react to an Irish woman who was obviously of African origin and driving a car packed full of personal belongings. He took a quick look at the document, then at me, the Brown woman, and finally into my packed car.

I expected suspicion and some formal questioning as to my intentions, but all he did was hand me back my passport and with a nod and a smile said:

"Welcome home."

What a wonderful feeling of belonging I experienced at that moment.

We should all be welcomed home irrespective of colour.

Sylvia Wohlfarth is a social anthropologist, teacher of English for Speakers of Other Languages, and intercultural dialogue facilitator. Her passion is to express herself in writing and raise awareness of the world's injustices, championing the marginalized and voiceless. She is driven by her love and humor. Half-Irish, half-Nigerian, Sylvia, born in Nigeria, now lives in Ireland after forty-two years in Germany.

UNDERSTANDING MICROAGGRESSIONS AND THEIR IMPACT 12

JESSE WILSON

A S A MIDDLE-AGED BLACK Britain, I have plenty of
experience of what it is like to live and move in spaces
where microaggressions are an all too frequent occurrence. The racism we know to exist today is a complex and
highly nuanced subject. Its complexity provides an unfortunate escape route for the many people who deny the full
extent of modern-day bigotry. Not all racists wear white
robes, bear swastikas, or are called Ken/Karen. For those
would-be allies who are aware we live in a society inherently constructed to oppress, the complexity becomes an

unfortunate barrier for navigating race and having those difficult conversations.

These difficult conversations are the ones we need to have if we truly want to alter the vector and avoid the pyramid of hate that often starts with microaggressions. Left unchecked, these first expressions quickly escalate and infect society, leading to further acts of bias and more aggressive forms of racism: systemic discrimination, violence, and ultimately genocide.

AN INTRODUCTION TO MICROAGGRESSIONS

If you need an example of a paradoxical misnomer, perhaps the word "microaggression" would adequately fit the bill. Micro to the recipient they invariably are not, although maybe to the aggressor. But the fact they are described as aggression correctly places value on their significance.

I imagine we all have ideas of what we mean by microaggressions and it is possible some of you may be thinking or at least have heard people say, "lighten up, it was only a joke," or "microaggressions are another example of buzzwords and political correctness gone amuck." The same people may also describe microaggressions as an example of "victimhood culture," called out by people who are overly sensitive or by people who wish to make a mountain out of a molehill. What they mean is, "I don't see a problem, and I don't understand why you are taking offence to something trivial —stiffen up and take it on the chin like the rest of us who have to deal with life."

Well, let me start by explaining with the best definition I have found for defining microaggressions and then give the reasons why we are wrong to trivialise any form of racism, even if the aggressor asserts it is a joke.

By definition, microaggressions are an acting out, consciously or otherwise, of a person's bias towards a marginalised group. The term was first used by Harvard University professor Chester M. Pierce back in the 1970s to describe the racial insults and slurs he had witnessed against Black people.

But here is the thing: microaggressions are not solely open insults and slurs. Perhaps this is why they are challenging to detect and understand, because they come in many different shapes and forms. They may be an openly hostile attack, a subtle dig, or derogatory comment expressed as a verbal, physical, or indirect participation in a racial fallacy. Whatever the form, the message is negative; the consequences are always felt and experienced as a reminder to the recipient they are not welcome, respected, or seen as equal.

JESSE
WILSON

PERSONAL EXAMPLES OF MICROAGGRESSION

Now that we have a definition, allow me to provide personal examples to help with our understanding. Before I do, let me just say I do not dwell on these examples; they have happened, and I have moved on. But if we are to have the difficult conversations, then we need to understand the impact and share the responsibility collectively.

In my lifetime I can't tell you the number of times I have had to respond to the question, "Where are you from?" On the surface, it may seem a perfectly innocuous and reasonable question to ask, and I would agree it does. The problem comes when I respond, as in my case, "I was born in Brighton, East Sussex." To which they reply, "No, I mean, where are you really from." I often say, playing ignorant but knowing precisely what they mean, "Oh you mean, where am I from, from." In answering, I would deliberately make the point that I was born in Britain, and my parents emigrated from Sierra Leone. To the aggressor, this often goes unnoticed. To me, it is a classic signal of the hidden meaning: Oh you can't be British, you are a foreigner, I see you as different.

Sometimes it is not the words that convey bias; nonverbal communication is just as informative, if not more. As a survival skill, a Person of Colour becomes well-attuned to detecting nonverbal cues that sometimes even the aggressor is unaware they are giving away.

One unfortunate example I can give occurred prior to where I live now. On the first day of moving into our new house, our then neighbour decided to do the neighbourly thing and introduce herself and offer help. My wife—like my then neighbour, a white female—initially opened the door and began what sounded like a pleasant and generous conversation.

After some time, my wife called out for me to say hello. So I stopped unpacking and walked into the hallway. In that instant, as my neighbour and my eyes met, I saw that all too familiar flicker of emotion and guessed at what she was thinking. Outwardly she was pleasant and said hello, but the look of disdain and lack of eye contact as she spoke had sufficiently betrayed her.

Noticing was enough, but we both continued the conversation as if what I had seen was nothing. For me, it was a precursor to meeting her husband, who reinforced what I had witnessed. In the time I knew them, I had to endure the occasional ignorant comments. Here are three paraphrased examples illustrating the spectrum of microaggressions.

- "You speak very well." – (microinsult) meaning I see you as a foreigner; you are an exception to commonly held stereotypes.
- "I don't see you as Black." – (microinvalidation) meaning I don't recognise and appreciate your ethnicity and experiences.
- "Black men are or have xxxx. No Offence." – (microassault) meaning its okay as a white person to comment/ tell a joke and justify the humour with these words.

Needless to say, as neighbours we rubbed along but I naturally learned to keep my distance because it was clear how they felt.

Surprisingly, intelligence does not make a white person immune to racism or a racist line of thinking. The prominent scientist James Watson, awarded the Nobel prize in 1962 for his role in the discovery of DNA's 'double helix,' is one such example. He is quoted as saying he was "inherently gloomy about the prospect of Africa" because "all our social policies are based on the fact that their intelligence is the same as ours—whereas all the testing says not really."

There is no scientific evidence to substantiate these

comments, and while Watson initially apologised after making the statement, he has since reiterated his original stance. Thankfully his peers and the scientific community have denounced his reckless and prejudicial opinions, but the damage has been done. I can recall to my dismay hearing a work colleague who I consider to be intelligent, quoting Watson and articulating similar views. So here you have an example of the power of influence and a reminder prejudice is not governed by intelligence or by facts, but by what we feel and believe to be true.

UNDERSTANDING
MICRO-
AGGRESSIONS
AND THEIR
IMPACT

As a Person of Colour, for better or worse, you are scarred by the memories of what it means to live and move in predominantly white spaces. Your first racial encounter teaches you to remain vigilant. Each racial microaggression is never experienced in isolation; they become layer upon layer of negative and harmful experiences that remind you because of your skin colour, so many inequalities and injustices exist.

The one thing you can always be sure about microaggressions is that the person at the receiving end is an individual, a human, a person who feels and deserves the right to feel safe and respected.

COMPREHENDING MICROAGGRESSIONS

People of Colour are sick and tired of being told we are the problem. We are tired of the disproportionate focus on the consequences of racism. We are tired of the side conversations that are distractions to the simple fact that what we deserve is an end to the notion and practice of white supremacy.

Controversial as it sounds, microaggressions are a practice of white supremacy. Now you may instantly argue that statement is blunt and brutal and needs to be tempered, especially given the knowledge some forms of bias are unconscious and unknown by the perpetrator. And for that, I would agree; but how do you account for the conscious, deliberate acts that thrive through a spectrum of aggressions and a distorted portrayal of People of Colour? You don't have to look far to see the failures to acknowledge the contributions to our collective history by People of Colour or to see the choice of language used in the media. Whenever a Person of Colour is in the limelight for a misdemeanour, we always know about their ethnicity!

JESSE WILSON

We all have biases and are capable of preserving aggressions against individuals and groups. After all, we are bombarded with images, stories, and information to support commonly held beliefs. Take, for example, if I asked you to think about Africa. What are the first thoughts that come to mind? I would be surprised if you said a vibrant, diverse continent with a long history of cultural contributions and plenty to still offer the world.

The issue is not that we are susceptible and have a bias; it is what we do with it that matters. When we fail to take the time and effort to understand individual perspectives, respect the complexity of race, and acknowledge the existence of inequalities, that is when we have problems.

Microaggressions are a manifestation of bias and a failure to comprehend individual perspectives—or quite simply put, an inability to show and have empathy towards a marginalised group.

It's a sad fact, but the pragmatist in me has come to accept racial bias and microaggressions will continue. There will always be individuals who will remain ignorant. They will continue to make racist choices because they believe they are protecting their heritage, their privilege, their supremacy.

For the first time in my lifetime, the topic of race is at the forefront of the minds of many people. The excuses so often used to avoid acknowledging there is a problem have worn thin. Circumstances today demand we all develop significant levels of cultural competency. The fact you are reading this book, this chapter, means that you are open, curious, willing to effect change, and ready to invest in your cultural competency. And that is a good thing.

Race and racism conversations are always going to be awkward because they are highly emotive subjects carrying with them a stigma, apprehensions over a visceral reaction, personal shame and guilt, and the immense weight of expectation.

So where and how do you begin? Well, as with any relationship, these conversations require work. You start with honesty and a desire to be a better person. You begin to show empathy by listening and accepting what may seem a contrary truth. You start with the understanding there is no quick fix, no blueprint, or a single solution. The minute we start generalising, we can guarantee we will be wrong.

A while back, I was on a long car journey, not because of the distance, but because of what was said by my then project manager, who openly admitted, "I would struggle

UNDERSTANDING MICRO-AGGRESSIONS AND THEIR IMPACT

with my daughter bringing home someone like you."
Immediately I knew what he meant, and I felt angry, hurt
and uncomfortable. But I had the presence of mind to ask
him to clarify. He explained as a father, he was scared for
his daughter and the ramifications she would face from
family and other members of their community. He feared
the abuse and the missed opportunities she and her children would endure.

He knew all too well the racial disadvantages and
injustices and understandably did not want them for his
daughter or family. In the confines of his car, though, this
one-sided conversation was beyond awkward. My project
manager, senior to me by both age and position, probably thought the power-dynamic would afford him space,
to be honest.

Part of me recognised that this may be an attempt at
honesty; part of me realised we were stuck in a car together.
But a more significant part of me was caught up in my
thoughts, thinking about how I felt and how I considered
his comments as racist. Naturally, my desire to keep the
peace and preoccupation with my thoughts meant there
was no meaningful dialogue.

DIMINISHING THE POWER IN MICROAGGRESSIONS

Despite the fact there is no simple solution to ending racism, there are three simple steps you can take if you want
to help lessen the power in microaggressions. The first step
involves conducting an honest appraisal of your own bias:
challenge yourself and recognise how we are always influenced by language and generalisations about groups of

people. The second step requires you to be active and call out microaggressions when you hear and see them. Support and reach out to the person who is affected. The third step is to increase your cultural awareness and continually pass that knowledge on. There is immense knowledge to be gained in building empathy and understanding.

In following these steps, think of it as if you were engaged in a long term relationship—be consistent, do the work, but most of all don't dwell in a sea of shame and guilt; it is not about you. It is not about who is right and who is wrong. Be prepared to get it wrong; be prepared for your friends of Colour to get it wrong. Understand we heavily influence each other every day by our words, actions, and inactions. It is a continual process to support, make space for the other, and understand differences. We, as members of society, have the chance to shape a future that is morally and ethically right. Empathy and understanding are our biggest asset against racism and the power given to microaggressions.

What we do with this opportunity will undoubtedly become a measure of our humanity in years to come. Will we collectively acknowledge and wash out the stain that is white supremacy, or will we reinforce and promote what we inherently know to be unjust.

Whatever we do, one thing I know for sure is that we mustn't hide from the difficult conversations and we mustn't afford microaggressions the power to alienate. For as much as we try to avoid the topic of race, it never goes away. It may quietly simmer for those not directly affected, but it bubbles, boils, and overspills in whatever available outlet for those who are impacted every day.

Jesse Wilson is a Charted Mechanical Engineer now IT professional, with a late passion for and love of writing. Since 2018, he has published poems and essays about equality, personal development, and happiness. As an active Masters athlete, he strives to live and fulfill his goal to be the best version of himself while inspiring others to do the same.

PART IV

ACHIEVING EQUALITY TOGETHER

YOU CAN KNOW ME 13

CHRISTIENNE L. HINZ

To my white allies:
    I do not speak for the African American community, a diverse and contentious group, regardless of the historical and contemporaneous experiences that we, its members, share. And it may be an error of judgement to offer my thoughts in open forum. Many self-described allies suffer a limited capacity for self-reflection and need to cultivate more deeply the art of circumspection before joining the conversation.

I choose, nevertheless, to speak to those white friends, neighbors, and family who have asked me, time and again, how to be "better allies," how to support my family and me through the upheaval of our current moment, and beyond. This is my partial reply.

We all can agree that America right now is experiencing a pivotal moment in racial history. People of color and our allies, a greater cross section of the American public than ever before, have come together to roar a definitive, "no!" to state-sponsored terrorism against its Black citizens.

Think of that shout as a unified and unifying musical composition—let's say a cantata—in opposition to 400 years of cumulative social, economic, racial, and juridical injustice. You and I—we—the composers, try various melodies, rhythms, voicing, and musical structures as we develop the score. Allow me to draw your attention to a refrain that I believe requires careful reconsideration.

The area of concern appears in the first movement of our score, in the very first stanza marked *molto pianissimo:* "White people can't know what it's like to be a Person of Color." Next stanza, *accentato:* "The Black experience has been uniquely torturous and is fundamentally incomprehensible to the white mind." Stanza three, *dolce,* "White Americans can never hope to understand Black pain and must never pretend empathy." Stanza four, *astinato:* "White can't know Black pain white can't know Black pain," closing with a repeat.

We have already agreed that Black voices must carry the composition's central melodies. We have agreed also that Black voices must order both rhythm and tempo. But the introduction of the white voice in the second bar of the first stanza is premature, contrived, and thoroughly unconvincing. The augmented 7th chord, with all of its violent, frightful, discordant tension, is a sound opening; and its inherent anxiety carries well across the entirety of the movement.

But why have we written white inability to comprehend or empathize with the Black experience into our "shared" composition? Where did this theme come from? Whose purpose and what purpose does it serve?

MANDATORY EMPATHY

CHRISTIENNE
L. HINZ

I find the notion that white friends and allies are incapable of understanding or empathizing with my experience as an African American astonishing, unnerving, and frankly unbelievable. There are very good reasons why this idea is part of Black discourse about race relations. Discourse has history; history is narrative, and narrative always operates at the nexus of competing claims to power. But discourse is not always and everywhere necessarily true. Black leaders and white people who try to respond to their cues about good allying, have accepted this discourse as truth outside of its history, outside of its purpose. This ready acceptance of white inability to either understand or empathize with the Black experience is one-part appropriate humility, one-part disingenuous genuflection, and three-parts structurally racist ideology that abrogates their responsibility to understand it and to empathize with it.

At best it is banal: no one can truly understand what it is to walk in another's shoes. At worst, it's another form of white Othering. It dehumanizes me. It dehumanizes you. It's lazy; it's a lie, and I want no truck with it.

Robert Frost argued that all knowing is metaphor. I agree. The Homo sapiens brain evolved for symbolic thinking and symbolic communication. Metaphor and simile are two of the most powerful hard-wired tools we use to explore, understand, navigate, communicate, and even create our world. To insist that humans stop using similes to understand each other is akin to asking us to willfully stop breathing. We can't.

Metaphors and similes are the chassis upon which we come-to-know. Mindfully crafting them is a necessary step in building human empathy. Empathy is altogether different from sympathy, which is of no interest to me. Pity's kissing-cousin requires neither knowing nor action. It merely greases social gears between indifferent strangers.

Empathy, on the other hand, has the power to convince you of your moral obligation to act in ways that are counter to your own and white self-interest, for the benefit of people of color. For me. If you want to convince me that Black lives matter, I require a more expensive and expansive investment on your part. I need you to be curious enough to seek to know me. I need you to convince me that my Black life matters to you.

If metaphor is the chassis enabling empathy, it also enables antipathy. White supremacy generates countless toxic metaphors in service to itself. And because metaphor is both communicable and heritable, its potential to metastasize cross-culturally and cross-generationally is very real. My daughter confidently informed me, when

166

she was eight years old, that she and her classmates agreed that Black people look like monkeys.

Be still. Don't react. *Just sit with that a moment.*

THE DELICATE POWER OF METAPHOR

Humans create metaphors, vile *and* sublime; these are by nature imperfect, but also infinitely elastic. They can be rejected, reconceived, rewritten, reformulated as many times as is necessary to enable richer knowing. Metaphors can engender sufficient empathy to drive moral conviction, which necessitates action. I need my allies to know me sufficiently for shared empathy. Knowing and empathy are lifelong processes rather than endpoints. Though perfect knowing is unattainable, I nevertheless insist that my allies take the journey. An example:

CHRISTIENNE
L. HINZ

I am your Black co-worker and we share office space. I have several pictures of my children on my desk, as do you. As cordial office mates, we admire each other's children, and laughingly commiserate over the trials of parenting—back-talk, fetid sneakers, chores left undone. I have my kids on speed-dial. You have your kids on speed dial. You rarely call them, though sometimes your youngest interrupts your day to ask for something trivial. You see me, however, furtively calling my son from my desk three or four times per day grilling him: "Where are you, who are you with, where are you going, how are you getting there, when are you coming home" and "You'd better call me when you get there."

You notice how frequently I excuse myself to the ladies room with red-rimmed eyes to repair my makeup, only returning to my desk when I have straightened my face. You know from watching television that Black parents live in terror for their children, their sons in particular. You have heard about "The Talk." You have seen depictions on television of weeping Black mothers trying to throw themselves onto the caskets of their lynched sons being lowered into the grave.

You don't know this experience personally, but you know that I am a mother caught in a riptide of fear, and that no matter how hard I swim, *I can't make my way to shore.*

You are not afraid for your children the way I am afraid for my children. You can't understand the experience of being afraid for them in the way or for the reasons I am afraid for mine. But don't you dare to tell me you don't know the feeling "caught in a riptide." You laid awake at night as a child. Every night, you strained to hear the sound of your father coming home. You knew by the jingle of his keys as he pushed them in the lock whether he was drunk or sober. A decade of your life was spent praying under the covers, heart jerking in your chest, that the man coming home to you was your Daddy, not the monster who sometimes wore his skin.

Don't you dare to tell me you don't know what it is to be caught in a riptide and can't swim back to shore.

Be still. Don't react. *Just sit with that a moment.*

What do you do with the metaphor once you sense "through a glass darkly"—as Paul tells us—the monstrous burden woven through my African American experience? Only this: hold it in your mouth, even if it makes you gag. Probe it with the tip of your tongue like a sore tooth, searching for holes. Feel its many textures. Taste

168

its complex flavors. Then *swallow* it. Nourishing or poisonous, your metaphor belongs to you. The only absolute thing your metaphor has allowed you to know about my Black experience is absolutely the only thing you may say to me: "How terrified you must feel. No one should live in terror that way."

Because the human brain comes to know by creating metaphors and similes about the world, not understanding the African American experience can't be a matter of white cognitive incapacity (which incidentally would be forgivable). It is a matter of sheer *will*, (meaning the failure to try is close to unforgivable). The question is whether whites are willing to expend the energy to identify poor similes, forge new metaphors, come to sufficient understanding of the Black experience, and then to act.

A cost-benefit analysis of choosing to know or *refusing* to know is a whites-only privilege. W. E. B. Du Bois was entirely correct when he wrote that Black people intimately understand white lives while whites remain wholly ignorant of the lives of Black folks. From the moment my ancestors were put in chains, their very survival pivoted on understanding morally incomprehensible but economically rational white industrialized terrorism. Every African American alive today is the descendant of Black people who figured out how to navigate a white world.

We understand the gamut of white experience: white hierarchy, white logic, white values, white ideology, white institutions, white feelings, white motivations, white fears, fetishes and fragility. If Black people can develop and refine metaphors to understand the white experience (in all of its constituent complexity, pain and privilege) how

CHRISTIENNE L. HINZ

is it that white people are excused from understanding the Black experience?

Systemic racism is structured to make white empathy for the Black experience intolerably expensive. Too much lucre, too much status, too much social capital. Working towards understanding the Black condition would require proximity (without which, racist metaphors proliferate); mindfulness (without which, racist metaphors remain unchallenged); and effort (without which new metaphors remain unwritten). Proximity, mindfulness, and effort enable increasing degrees of empathy; but empathy, itself, isn't free.

When white people feel the power of the metaphor "caught in a riptide," when they understand that the riptide was created to profit their ancestors, when they realize that they, themselves, profit from it still, then white people are forced to face their moral obligation to do something about institutional racism. Empathy is a threat to white supremacy; the very threat segregation is structured to prevent. I *require* my allies to resist the seduction of segregated empathy.

KALEIDOSCOPIC "BLACK EXPERIENCES"

While the belief that whites are unable to understand the Black experience serves white privilege, it is also a technique of Black cultural, political, and personal self-defense. White people regularly deploy false-equivalencies and fake empathy to invalidate the Black experience of racism, and our right to express our pain and outrage in white spaces. Perhaps you have heard, or perhaps you, yourself, have said to Black acquaintances, "Managers who follow you around stores aren't racist. It happens to me all the time!"

White ignorance of the Black experience of racism is as real as it is intentional. This ignorance builds, services, and elides the reality of the privileges they enjoy under a white supremacist regime. It is critical for Black people to name white ignorance in order to insist on the reality of our suffering, and the legitimacy of our demands for justice.

The claim that whites are unable to understand the Black experience is also one of the ways that African Americans combat the self-hatred or self-doubt that is a painful consequence of living with white hegemony. To love ourselves, our children, and one another, we must actively reject toxic depictions of Black life produced by white racist ideology. "You don't know me. You can't know me," is a bold and necessary resistance to the painful impact of the hegemon's gaze, which has defined, colonized, criminalized, pathologized, commodified, appropriated, and monetized Black bodies for 400 years.

CHRISTIENNE
L. HINZ

Lastly, the notion that whites are unable to understand the Black experience depends upon a rigidly narrow, monochromatic view of the constitutive elements of that experience. If the sum total of the Black experience in America has been the historical, cumulative, and immediate impact of white supremacy—our suffering, struggle, and inevitable death, as narrated by both conservatives and liberals, then indeed, it is true that white Americans can never know anything about the Black experience.

However, the Black experience in America is not and has never been monochromatic—white Hollywood, white publishers, white editors, and self-appointed Black speakers for the Black community be damned. I am Black all day every day. In addition to struggling with institutional racism while Black, I am a middle-class, cis-gender woman, a feminist, bisexual Quaker in an interracial heterosexual marriage, an incest survivor, and I suffer a number of PTSD-related mental illnesses. I have had two abortions. I am mother to two brilliant biracial neuro-atypical children. Over the course of my life, I have lived in poverty, received Aid to Families with Dependent Children, become a Master Gardener, competed successfully in equestrian and Nordic sport. I have declared bankruptcy. I can field dress a deer. I am a ceramicist, a fiber-artist, a writer of poetry and fiction, a composer, fluent in Japanese language and culture, a gamer, a history professor, and I happen to play Roller Derby.

What white mother, watching her son score that first touchdown of the season, can claim not to understand a Black mother's exhilaration watching her son do the same? What white father, tumbling into love while gazing into his newborn's face, can claim not to understand a Black father's tumble into love when he does the same? White people can and are normatively expected to empathize with joyful Black experiences. But joy is not a whites-only gated community where Black people sometimes visit but excuse themselves before the dinner hour. I scorn racist paradigms to the contrary.

Suffering is not a Black ghetto through which white people drive with car windows tightly rolled shut and doors locked. I repudiate racist claims to the contrary. The Black experience is one of *life*, not death. It is a human experience; and Black people of all walks are busy trying to live life in the best way they know how. Whites who can't find an intersection with which to come to know Black lives *aren't looking*.

I don't expect every white ally to understand all of my lived experiences. I don't understand all of theirs. I do expect every white ally to be curious enough to look for the intersections between our lived experiences, use that material to explore metaphors, develop empathy, build trust, and then act on the moral obligations that grow out of understanding the difficulties I carry as an African American. It is what I do for them.

I had a telling experience last year, at the parent orientation to my daughter's private school. During the mandatory stale cookie and warm Kool-Aid hour, a white woman rushed up to me, and without telling me her name or asking mine, gushed, "I'm so glad to know you and your daughter will be part of our community! I have been advocating to create a more diverse student body and so I wanted to extend you a special welcome, and to thank you for choosing to send her here. I know it isn't cheap. If you or your daughter have any diversity problems while you're here, come see me. I'm the diversity person!"

Up until that moment, I had been having a very Black experience. I was politely putting a stale cookie in my mouth, washing it down with warm Kool-Aid, and wondering how long I had to remain at the meeting to satisfy the rules of politeness. Race as an institutional diversity point was clearly more salient to this woman's experience of my Blackness than it was to my own. The parameters of her "alliance" with me extended no further than the utility of a few millimeters of black skin she tried

CHRISTIENNE
L. HINZ

to snatch off my back and cram into her hand-stitched "diversity" pocketbook.

Did she really believe that the way *she* valued my Blackness would make *me* feel valued? "These cookies are terrible, but I don't bake. Do you?" would have been a far better way to express interest in me and to demonstrate that my Black Life Mattered to her. Inclusivity performance is a diseased branch grafted to the same old white racist rootstock planted in the same old white supremacist orchard where Black bodies are pruned to meet the needs of white hegemony.

You can't be my ally without feeling curious about my lived human experience. I won't trust you with the portion of that experience that is suffering, rage, powerlessness, battle, and hope unless and until you have real sweat equity invested in locating and exploring intersections between our lived human experiences. You can't understand sufficiently Black life *in extremis* without doing the labor to write the metaphors that will allow us to know each other sufficiently. If you don't know me sufficiently, you will be the "ally" who hands me a wet match when what I asked for is your inferno. To merely recite "Black Lives Matter" is nothing more than self-aggrandizing performance if you don't empathize with a Black life that matters to you. You can't be my ally if you don't know me.

RECOMPOSING HARMONY

So, let's reconsider the cantata we have chosen to compose together. Let us name the first movement, "Dialogue." As previously agreed, Black voices hold the melody; they also drive rhythm and tempo. As in our first attempt, we boldly lance America's historical wound, with all of its suppurating lethality, using that unbearable augmented 7th interval. *Molto agitato:* the melody a heavily syncopated shout. Wait to add the white voice. Wait . . . wait . . . Be patient. We can hint at a potential harmonic resolution with the white voice, stutter our way toward rationalized syncopated and contrapuntal rhythms. But not yet: make the white voice work for it.

Dialogue is best begun with questions. Should the invitation to dialogue emerge from the Black melody? Or should it emerge as a dissonance from the white voice's attempt to harmonize? Which questions will be asked? To my white allies, I say you choose. You take the risk of asking the wrong question at the right time, or the right question at the wrong time. You bear the discomfort of revealing, facing, and dismantling your own privileged ignorance.

CHRISTIENNE L. HINZ

After 400 years of shouting our stories into a hurricane of white denial, disbelief, and co-optation, white allies should not be surprised when people of color respond to white questions with sarin-saturated silence, or the flat accusation, "you can't understand the Black experience. Don't pretend you can. Don't even try." If we actually believed this, we would be no more angry or contemptuous of your efforts than we are of dogs who can't learn to speak English. But we are angry. And contemptuous. And tired.

Take the risk as well as the lumps that come with learning to ask better questions. Questions of *curiosity*: "What is your name? Who are your people? Where do you come from? What gods speak to you?" Questions of *opening:*

Will you come to my table? Will you share your family's secret recipe? Would you like me to help you weed your garden? Would you stitch your name on my quilt?" *Observant* questions: "Why are you weeping? Why is there thunder on your brow?" *Transformative* questions: "How can I change myself to help you? How can I change the circumstances to help you?" Questions of *offering:* "Would you like me to walk your grandmother to church? Should I stand behind you, at your side, or put my body in front of yours? Can I dress your wounds? Do you need me to hide your children in my closet?" *Human* questions: "Will you let me hold your heart?"

No knowing no empathy.
No empathy no action.
No action no justice.
No justice no peace.

YOU CAN
KNOW ME

Christienne L. Hinz, Ph.D. is the daughter of a surgical nurse, the granddaughter of a cook, the great-grand-daughter of a laundress, the great-great granddaughter of a teacher and the great-great-great granddaughter of a midwife emancipated from slavery. She earned a Ph.D. in modern Japanese history from Ohio State University, the second African American woman in the United States to do so.

SO YOU WANT TO HELP: LET'S GET MOVING!

14

SHERRY KAPPEL

H ERE WE ARE. IF you've made it to this chapter, chances are you are feeling slightly overwhelmed. Few, if any, People of Color live without experiencing acts of racism. But a lot of us white folks living and working in our lily-white worlds can go blissfully unaware of it for long periods of time. In fact, you've probably assumed numerous times that Black people were exaggerating their claims! And then, bam—2020 hits, and we're discovering that racism isn't just as bad as they said, it's far worse. It's ugly, it's everywhere, it's in more than half the people we know and love.

We cannot call ourselves caring citizens or kind human beings if we continue to watch from the sidelines. So this is where the rubber hits the road. Except, ahem, what exactly does that mean? Some of the other chapters have hinted at or touched upon a lot of the options, but this chapter will provide explicit steps you can take to help eradicate racism and build equality.

BE A CARING PERSON

Being the best person you can be isn't the only prerequisite to being a good ally, but it's the most important (to many things, really!). If you did nothing more than understand the problem and fight the racism within yourself, you will have made it further than a significant portion of the population. However, I'm willing to bet that if you do get that far, you won't be able to tolerate the injustices you see around you. First steps first, though.

STUDY UP After you've read this book, read it again. Read a variety of books and articles by Black, Indigenous, and People of Color (BIPOC). Follow some of them on social media. This is for numerous reasons. Obviously, racism is deep and complicated, and has permeated every aspect and every level of our culture. You could study it for decades, as I have, and find there's still more to learn. White people aren't on the receiving end of racism, so we won't ever be experts. I learn new things literally every other day.

Beyond that, here is how the cycle has historically

worked. Black people explain racism and their pain. White people say, Nah, no way! Eventually some white people become partially aware of the racial injustice taking place in their midst and ask their Black friends to educate them, who reiterate racism and their pain. The white person finds it all hard to believe, it conflicts with their own interests, and/or they don't think it's their problem to solve and walk away. Wash, rinse and repeat. Is it any wonder that after hundreds of years of this, many Black folks are too frustrated, angry, and sad to tell us all yet again? Most times, even close Black friends will avoid these discussions, or when pressed, they might placate us by saying "you're fine, you're not like the others" because the trust simply isn't there. And who can blame them? Fortunately, we have the internet at our disposal, so let's keep googling and stop pleading with our Black friends to do our homework for us.

SHERRY KAPPEL

The more you know about racism, the more you will notice it all around you. Why does the media talk about "Black-on-Black crime," for example, but never "white-on-white crime"? Does a magazine use mostly or all white models? If so, why have we simply been conditioned to accept that? Does your HR recruiter always choose the white candidates because they are more qualified or is he simply more comfortable with them? The more you know about racism, the more you will recognize it—study up, and open your eyes.

LISTEN AND FOLLOW I don't know if it's common to all humans, unique to Americans, or a sign of our times, but we are not good listeners, even with our closest friends. Often, we listen just long enough to develop our responses, or for confirmation of our own world views. For white people, this is frequently apparent in our conversations with Black friends and coworkers, even when discussing race—as Stephen Matlock demonstrates so well in Chapter 10.

The truth is, we will never understand racism like a Black person does, or the pain that it inflicts. Nor will we ever have the level of experience Black people do in fighting for their rights and knowing which tactics work and when. Beyond that, it is, well, just plain rude for a white person (or anyone for that matter) to try to define not only a Black, Indigenous, or Person of Color's reality—but anyone's, especially when the former is part of the group that has inflicted the pain on the latter. You might be well read and have the best of intentions, but never has it been more important to simply listen and absorb.

Similarly, white people who have always been encouraged to lead, must learn to follow for a change. Not just because Black people have more experience demanding justice, but because we need to begin sharing power and establishing trust. An excellent example of this is with the Women's March over the past several years, where white women in many cities shut out their Black sisters from planning and speaking. Now, at a time when all women need as much political support as they can get, BIPOC women are justifiably wary of participating.

ACKNOWLEDGE YOUR OWN RACISM AND PRIVILEGE
Hopefully it's been clear in the previous chapters how none of us can avoid having racial biases; it is simply far too ingrained in our culture, in places we don't even think

to look. White people shouldn't feel bad or guilty about acknowledging this, as long as we're working to improve ourselves. (Note: some white people love to respond that BIPOC are also racist; the difference is that white people are in power while Black people are struggling for their very lives.) Working to understand racism and recognizing our biases will also help Black people to trust us.

Related to this, learn the benefits of apologizing if you haven't already. This is another area where too many people have been fed a lie: being right, for some reason, all too often takes precedence over learning and growing from our mistakes. Just apologize! And even if you aren't personally responsible for something, you can be sympathetic that it happened. I have benefited from white privilege my entire life, even though I didn't ask for it, and I'm very sorry that others haven't had the same opportunities, so—I apologize. It suggests empathy and helps in building that trust.

MAKE SOME BLACK FRIENDS Last but not least, we white folks need to get outside of our monochromatic suburbs and our comfort zones to widen our circle of friends. Shop at some Black-owned businesses (which also helps to advance economic equality), visit a Black church, volunteer with the NAACP. As Christienne Leigh Hinz notes in Chapter 14, you can't truly be an ally to a "race" till you're an ally to someone you care about It's personal. Do the work to be trustworthy: again, listen, demonstrate true concern, and open yourself up to other world views. Because the irony is, when you embrace the differences that have been used to divide us, you discover we're all the same in the ways that matter.

Of course, you don't need to write a dissertation on Blackness or join a Black church before you can start doing the work of an ally. You needn't be an expert to speak out and lend your support to Black communities and causes. Most Black people know we are relatively clueless about racism and forgive the occasional error if you're fighting the good fight (although that's not a license to show up completely uninformed). Conversely, however, white silence is complicity with the status quo of racism. That is what keeps it going. So, for anyone with their heart in the right place, the work needs to start now.

SO YOU WANT TO HELP: LET'S GET MOVING!

The good news is that there are many, many ways in which an ally can help—we all have different skill sets and something to offer. Here are just a few suggestions.

GET POLITICAL Get out and vote—Every. Single. Election! As Civil Rights leader and U.S. Representative John Lewis noted in *The New York Times*, "Voting and participating in the democratic process are key. The vote is the most powerful nonviolent change agent you have in a democratic society. You must use it because it is not guaranteed. You can lose it."

Don't just vote for the national tickets but also the local ones; oftentimes these are for the positions that have the most immediate effect on our day-to-day lives. And white people, don't just vote for whomever sounds good to you, listen to who your Black friends support. Ask them why. As a minority, there aren't enough Black people to effect major change. White folks and all People of Color need to put in a vote for the equality of every citizen; it's as American as baseball and apple pie.

Between elections, get to know your legislators and how they vote. Contact them when you strongly agree—or disagree. Contact them again. And again. While most politicians vote along party lines, there is plenty of activity behind the scenes that you can affect as a constituent, especially when an official is up for re-election. Some organizations will even provide a template for you to edit, and an easy mechanism for hitting all of your legislators at once simply by entering your zip code. Google it. Sharing your views has never been easier.

One more option? Run for office! I'm not kidding. All sorts of political neophytes are fed up with the assorted inequalities and jumping on the ballot. If you are an extrovert with strong opinions, give it some thought.

BE VOCAL Express your views among family and friends, and on social media; let others know how you feel and why, provide details and examples, and share ways to help. If there's an article or website you found particularly useful, include a link when you can. People complain about all the political commentary in their newsfeeds, but the truth is that friends and family have a lot more influence on a person's opinions than any other source. Although Black Lives Matters is several years old, the organization received unprecedented levels of support this year when white people took to Facebook, Instagram, and Twitter to express their outrage over George Floyd, Breonna Taylor, and Ahmaud Arbery. Go to *Change.org* and similar websites to sign petitions and share them.

WRITE OR SPEAK AS APPROPRIATE IN PERSONAL SITUATIONS, AS WELL Support anti-racism efforts at your company. Talk to your congregation, or your quilting group. Reach out to Black coworkers and acquaintances to let them know that you care, you have some idea how they might be feeling about what's going on in the country, and ask how you might help them. Similarly, amplify Black voices. Remember that as an ally our job is to help them be heard, not to own the narrative of their experience. If a Black friend is willing, perhaps they're the better option to speak to your congregation. Be a facilitator.

In particular, respond when you hear racist statements or see racist acts! I know this one can be tough, because often these moments are instigated by our friends, family, and coworkers. If a Black person is present, your first concern should be their safety, just as it would be with any victim of an attack. But also bear in mind the old saying that — as long as a Black person isn't in direct physical danger—honey goes further than vinegar when confronting people about racist comments or acts. Anger rarely changes a person's mind. Be clear and direct, and use your communication skills to help them understand why they're wrong: "I used to feel the same way, but then I learned that . . ." Perhaps take them aside, so they're not publicly embarrassed. Re-read Chapter 16 by Clay Rivers. It gets easier the more you do it.

PUT YOUR MONEY WHERE YOUR MOUTH IS Donate any extra money you might have to the Black Lives Matter movement, the NAACP, or wherever you feel comfortable. A lot of us are pinching pennies right now, but if everybody gave even so much as their spare change, think how that would add up. Or help a protestor make bail!

As mentioned before, also be a patron of Black businesses, restaurants, and artists. The best way to raise up a community is to share your appreciation of their contributions and help them raise themselves up. And what better way to avoid cultural appropriation than to go directly to the source? On the flip side, remember to vote with your wallet. If a store or restaurant is known for providing poor service to its non-white customers, there are typically plenty of alternatives who would appreciate your business.

Additionally, use your clout in the places where you have influence. If you're the president of your school's PTA or hold a leadership position at your church, synagogue, or mosque, I can assure you that the school or house of worship will be interested in your opinion. Are there organizations where you provide money or volunteer? It's their business to care what you think! Right now, all sorts of companies are declaring their undying support for Black Lives Matter, and it's not just because they finally grew a heart—they're after your wallet.

PUT YOURSELF OUT THERE Show up at a rally or protest! I know this one sounds a little scary right now, especially if you follow the media closely (their job is to highlight the extreme moments, after all) but I promise that the vast majority are peaceful events filled with friendly people who will appreciate your being there. Also, be aware that much of the violence is perpetrated by fake protesters who want the cause to look bad, and most of it happens at night. I have attended numerous events, as have my daughters and their friends, and we all find them to be very friendly, educational, and uplifting. It's also a lot of fun to fulfill your inner creator by creating a sign, and kids love to participate.

LET'S GET MOVING!

Still with me? Yay! Yes, the list is long. If we each do our part, though, we will get there—our country's heart and soul is at stake, so failure is not an option. As Former First Lady Michelle Obama noted in her first Podcast, "We are each other's brothers and sisters' keepers. It is not enough that I succeed on my own ... I have to care about the kid in the desk next to me." And yes, change is scary. Some of these activities may seem a little scary. On the flip side, you will meet many amazing people!

America has always claimed to be a melting pot, the land of opportunity, a place with "justice and liberty for all." What Black people—all People of Color—simply want, is the chance to get a good education. To be healthy. To live in the best neighborhood for their family. To be the best person they can possibly be. In other words, the same things white people, all human beings, want. Let's make the American dream a reality and help our fellow countrymen get there.

Sherry Kappel is a poet, essayist, and fiction writer with an MFA from the University of Pittsburgh. She looks for the best in humanity and is driven by empathy in her writing and in life. Her work is on Medium, where she also edits *Snapshots*, the *Haiku Hub*, and special projects for *Our Human Family*. Sherry lives in North Carolina with her husband, daughters, and critters.

TALKING WITH PEOPLE ABOUT RACISM

15

CLAY RIVERS

H AVING READ *FIELDNOTES ON ALLYSHIP* this far, you're more familiar with the precise nature of racism, the forces that maintain systemic racism, and how to prepare to do the work of allyship, equality, and anti-racism, than you were before. And you probably feel that what you once thought of as unknowable or unattainable is now very much within your grasp. Great!

Now what?

You go out into the world and you talk to people. And you walk your talk. But before you start stamping out racism everywhere you see it, know that you're going flail around on the floor like a newborn in your first attempts at being an ally. Now that you know what microaggressions are, one day you'll find yourself in the grocery store, the gas station, or the mall and you'll see a microaggression unfold before your very eyes. The impudent salesperson or cashier will dole out a heaping of disdain to an undeserving customer of color, as described in this book. You'll note that customer try to shrug off the cashier's callous display of racism as they leave. The moment will catch you so off guard you may stand there like a deer transfixed by the headlights until the cashier cheerfully calls you to the register. Cue: sad sax riff.

Fail.

Don't worry, racism never takes a day off. Unfortunately, there will be thousands of opportunities for do-overs. In time you'll crawl, stand up for an instant, take a step or two, stumble, and fall before you're able to walk, run, or even sprint. Learning how to handle situations is a process, but that's where the joy is: in the learning and doing. Trust me.

And why should you trust me? Because I'm a multi-discipline expert in confronting misconceptions. I've been Black every day of my life for over fifty years and during those fifty-plus years, my friends, I've been in a variety of situations in predominantly white spaces, and in every single one of those situations I've been Black. I attribute my longevity in part to knowing the ways of white people and how to navigate those spaces. It incumbent upon me— and all Black people—to know the ways of white people. The hollow smile, the false laughter, and the "Sure, I'll take care of that," that heralds betrayal. Our lives depend on knowing those ways and have for 400 years. Truth be told, lest I sound pompous, I attribute my longevity to the grace of God which has kept me from encountering hardcore racists who despise my blackness so much that they would seek to do me harm.

Now add to the mix, the irrefutable fact that I am forty-eight-inches tall. *Bet you didn't see that coming!* I'm not going to belabor the topic, but the takeaway here is that between people's reactions to my ethnicity and disability (dwarfism), I've got more than enough experience with being "othered" dealing with people's preconceived notions of what a Black man living with dwarfism is capable and incapable of. The upside is that I've had countless opportunities to either fold under pressure or transcend other's prejudices, as well as my own. The vast majority of the time, I choose the latter. With that said, I might have a useful tip or two for you. Now let's get to work.

TRUTH AND LOVE

These two commodities—and I refer to them as commodities because they're precious and not enough people have enough of either—are at the core, outer edges, and middle of serving as an ally. By standing up for BIPOC (no need to spell this one out anymore) in America or POC (this one either) around the world, you are committing an act of love by speaking the truth against the lies of racism. I'm not massaging your ego or touting how "good" or "moral" you are for traveling this road. I'm giving you the facts. When your compassion moves you to intercede on behalf of someone else, that's love. Plain and simple. Countering racist thoughts, words, and deeds—which we know are rooted in irrational and unfounded beliefs—with facts extinguishes those lies with truth.

When you commit to serving as an ally, instances of racism become more and more apparent. And I'm not suggesting you go out in search of a boogeyman behind every tree. The truth is, once you see the humanity in someone, you can never unsee it. So it stands to reason that when you see someone attempt to deny another person's humanity or deny them the respect they are due by virtue of their inherent humanity, it will impact you negatively. On a visceral level.

Your words and actions will have the biggest impact on people you already know. Why? Because you already have an existing relationship with them. There's a given level of trust that comes with any relationship. Your family, friends, and coworkers are more likely to take what you say to heart than a complete stranger. For most of us, though, engaging family members about polarizing topics is like walking through a minefield, and rightfully so. Who wants to be accused of ruining Thanksgiving all because we took the bait and dropped a truth bomb on a parent, aunt, or uncle who's in their cups? Which brings us to the next point—

TIMING

Timing is everything. There have been countless well-intentioned people who, in the name of allyship, have launched themselves into situations at the wrong time and have set their relationship and reputation with the people they hoped to serve ablaze as a cautionary tale of how not to be an ally. Allyship requires that you assess the truth of a situation. Does the marginalized BIPOC need/want my assistance? Is it the right time to respond? Is it the right setting? Is it better to confront someone over racist words or actions in the heat of the moment, or would it be better to wait and speak to them privately at a time when they're more apt to actually listen to what you have to say? These are determinations you'll have to make on your own because there's no one size fits all prescription for dealing with people and there are too many variables in play. **Always try to make the best decision possible for those whose interests you're supporting in any given moment without putting anyone in danger.** But I guarantee you, with time, you'll get better at assessing situations and determining when it's a good time to get involved and when not.

When advocating for equality, you're not offering people help with a check-out-line impulse purchase of a Snickers bar over a bag of Skittles. And you're not selling them a car. Via your words and actions, you're presenting a different way, a broader way, to see the world and everyone in it. Ultimately, you're asking them to subscribe to confidence and not fear. Truth and not lies. Love and not hate. One thing that is easy to lose sight of is that people don't come to hold racist beliefs overnight. Hatred isn't an online course they completed in six weeks. People mimic the behavior they see. And the longer they live in that environment, the more entrenched those beliefs become. No matter how desperately we want people to stop doing

195

and saying racist things once and for all, truth is, it ain't gonna happen that fast. Never does. Paradigm shifts occur gradually over time with increased understanding. Think about how long it took you to change your thinking about any number of topics.

SEEDING AND WEEDING

Think of *your* actions as planting and nurturing seeds, and pulling out weeds. Seeding is anything that encourages a budding mindset that embraces racial equality. (See activities in the preceding chapter.) Weeding can be thought of as responding to a racist comment and can consist of expressing displeasure, pointing out inappropriateness, or expressing truth that neutralizes racist statements. Use your best judgment as to whether it's best to speak up or remain silent in a given moment. I don't recommend that anyone put themselves in physical danger. Nor am I giving specific phrases to use as they are not magic words that will repel or compel an anti-racist mindset; what works for one person may not work for another.

For some people, it will take weeks, months, or even years before they finally come around and it sinks in. I write that not to give them a license to ill, but to remind you to breathe. Remembering this reinforces the notion that you don't have to "fix" anyone. You can't fix anyone. The decision to change is solely that individual's choice. I firmly believe that people can change. I say this because I know it can happen. I've seen it happen too many times to think it's a freak accident. I know a number of people who grew up in patently racist homes who later discovered

196

they were sold a false bill of goods about Black people and People of Color. The reality of their firsthand experience with People of Color didn't match up with the negative stereotypes they were taught to believe. It's a pretty profound experience to find that your perception of the world is wrong, and that of the people who taught you is woefully incorrect. These folks were forced to reconcile the difference between the two and did so at their own pace. People can change when they want to change, when they believe change is possible, and when they know how to change.

There's no sanctioned, universal infographic (that I know of) that maps the transition from a racist to an anti-racist worldview a person can point to say, "I used to be a Two, but now I'm at Step Four." At the same time as you can't say with surety, "Me? I've reached a 75% success rate in allyship." It's a process, full of ups and downs, hits and misses, gaffes, a few laughs, and successes. If you're lucky, you'll forge new relationships with like-minded people along the way. In the meantime, all you can do is keep nurturing those anti-racist seeds and snatching out those pesky weeds. Chances are you aren't the only person speaking to them about their beliefs. As an ally, you don't have to be present when the fruit ripens. It's more important to do what you can to help those anti-racist seeds take root. Yours and those of others.

CLAY RIVERS

TALKING WITH BIPOC ABOUT RACISM

Now more than ever, people are talking about equality and race, but in order for two people of different ethnicities to have a productive conversation about racism, two

197

mutually agreed upon prerequisites must be in practice—

1. Speaking to one another with respect and care for the other person's inherent humanity
2. Actively listening with the intent to leave the dialogue with a better grasp of the other person's point of view

—without these two conventions, even with the best intentions, the conversation will invariably morph into a shouting match with one person feeling marginalized and the other personally attacked. One factor that makes discussions of racial equality difficult is that some white people can't accept the fact that a BIPOC's firsthand experience is both valid and real. Why? The short answer: because it's so different from their own.

A couple of years ago, I spoke about race with a very good white friend of mine. He is as far removed from the racial tension we seen on TV as anyone can be. His lifestyle is what anyone would refer to as upper-middle class. He has an open mind and based on our friendship of more than three decades, I can state the guy is no racist. A few days after our first in a series of in-depth conversations about race relations in America, he informed me that while I made no implied or direct accusation that he was a racist, my friend said he felt personally attacked. This has been a common response from most of my white male friends. I informed him that our discussion of racism, bias, white privilege, and how they're manifested by actual hooded, cross-burning racists, homegrown vigilantes, or Neo-Nazis was in no way an accusation of being a racist, nor was it a personal attack. I explained that I was communicating my firsthand encounters with racism. Without providing a transcript of the conversations, we moved forward in our understanding of one another and the issues at hand.

SNOW

This is going to sound really crazy at first, but it's 200 percent true: No Black, Indigenous, or Person of Color owes anyone an explanation of their experience with racism or justification for why they feel the way they do. Full stop. Granted, such a conversation can be beneficial, but curiosity does not outrank self-preservation. Living a life in the face of an onslaught of everything from microaggressions to murder is exhausting. And traumatizing. Society doesn't poke and prod victims of violent crimes or trauma to relive their experiences. "Hey, can you tell me about that time 'x' happened. Yeah, I know it may have been harrowing, but I'd *really* like to know what that was all about." It's rude, wrong, and an assault on human dignity. Don't do it. Be forewarned, the response you receive may cut you off at the knees.

Would that be considered a "nice" response? No, but neither is racism. Is it appropriate? Yes. Maintaining one's boundaries and self-dignity occasionally requires a firm admonition to those who would overstep said boundaries. If a BIPOC does invite you into such a conversation about their experience with racism, *listen* with the intent to develop a better understanding of their experience. Don't question their interpretation or ask if they're "sure" things happened the way they described. This is not a bridge to increased understanding. If anything, it throws

CLAY
RIVERS

up roadblocks and signals a lack of belief that the BIPOC is incapable of comprehending their own experience and adds actual insult to injury.

For those of you who doubt the stories of BIPOC about what they've experienced, I offer you this hashtag to remember: #snow. Imagine you've lived your entire life in a tropical climate and you've never heard of, seen, or experienced snow. One day someone who lives in an arctic climate tries to explain the concept of winter, snow, blizzards, and all that comes with snow in the winter. Your lack of experience with snow does not negate the existence of snow, the need for winter clothing, the accumulation of snowdrifts, and blizzards. To entertain the notion that snow exists, you have to concede that the world as you know and have experienced it is not the only way the world can exist.

A friend learned of an incident he suspected was rooted in racial inequity that happened to me, and said, "I can't imagine how deeply that affected you, but I understand what it's like to be human; to feel discounted, mistreated, and misunderstood. I'm here for you." Those last four words opened the door to a deeper conversation about the incident.

GUARD YOUR HEART AND OTHER BODY PARTS

To say serving as an ally is challenging is an understatement, but it is rewarding work. You're bound to encounter people who aren't interested in what you have to say about equality and racism—of all ethnicities. Fear of change and what life will be like after the change are prime inhibitors of paradigm shifts. People will lash out or they may get physical. We're neither condoning nor encouraging physical violence. That does nothing for marginalized people, their causes, or you. Don't take terse responses personally even though you are the person on the receiving end of those remarks. Their actions say more about their state of mind than yours.

First and foremost, neither I nor any of the authors in this book recommend that you put yourself in harm's way. But if you're a six-foot-four, two-hundred-and-fifty-pound guy with hands the size of glazed hams, and you feel your size and presence will lessen the likelihood of someone causing a scene, that's on you. Just make sure you respond *wisely*, and not hastily.

Personally, I think of myself as an accidental activist. Not all that long ago, I dreamed of resurrecting the romantic-comedy genre by writing the greatest screenplay of all time. Hey, priorities change. It may seem as if I fell into "this," but I like to think Providence has led me here. I'm not one for demonstrations. It's not that I think they're unimportant. Demonstrations are the bedrock of this country's founding, but they're not for me. At forty-eight inches tall, large numbers of people coupled with up-close and personal views of people's butts and elbows are overwhelming and undesirable. So that's not my thing.

But I've found other outlets that are better suited to me and my abilities that still have an impact. Not to toot my own horn, but I always enjoyed writing. Years ago, I wrote an essay in response to conversations I had with non-Black friends about racism. Much to my surprise, the essay caught fire (the good kind) and led to many more.

Those essays led to the creation of an online publication where I encountered more people with their own experiences and desire for a more racially equitable world which led to founding a nonprofit, and now this book.

I mention all of the above to say, fear not. There's no way you can possibly know how your efforts can positively impact the world. You don't need to. Despite all the do's and don'ts, this isn't about being what we call serving the world as an "ally." It's infinitely larger than that. All of this is about being better humans and can be summed up in three words: Love one another.

Clay Rivers is an author, award-winning art director, accidental activist, president of the nonprofit organization Our
Human Family, Inc. and founder and editorial director of
the Medium publication of the same name. Both the nonprofit and the publication reflect one of his core beliefs:
People change when they *want* to change, when they *know*
change is possible, and when they know *how* to change.

THE ROLE OF PROTESTS 16

AISHA PAZ

My FAMILY IS WHAT people call "conformist." I was not raised in a model family. My grandfather left my grandmother and she raised her children alone in a poor and remote neighborhood. My mom got pregnant as a teenager and had to work, so I was raised by my aunts and my grandmother. But the fact that we were conformists made us neutral to most situations around us. If you were a neighbor, you probably would have no other adjective to describe my family than "normal." We leave early to get to work or school, we don't live in luxury or poverty, we don't spend too much time on the street, we don't turn on the loud music at home, we don't drink or use drugs; we always go out with our IDs in our pockets, and we don't argue in public. We are above suspicion. And so are most families in the world. The problem is that we have given up a lot to be seen as ordinary. We've preferred to ignore in order to be ignored. Unsuspected by unemployment, hunger, violence . . . to ignore has been to be passive. Be passive about injustice, violence, prejudice, intolerance. We were passive to avoid getting into trouble.

But getting into trouble is not just up to you.

The recognition process can be quite difficult. Most of the time, we just don't want to accept that people are simply mean and "that's all there is about them, period." We are human. It is normal to reject that people in general "are bad, period." It is normal to reject that people we know "are bad, period." It is in our nature to believe in the best of people. And so, we create vain excuses to justify intolerable attitudes. "It was a dangerous place . . . " "She asked for it . . . " "He looked suspect . . . " and the classic "A few bad apples." The last sentence was the same used to justify the biggest slaughter in Fortaleza, Brazil, the seventh most dangerous city in the world. My home.

ELEVEN

On the night of November 11, 2015, eleven people were murdered and seven others were injured in Curió, a neighborhood of my city. The crimes took place in less than six hours. Forty-four rotten apples were involved. I was thirteen and had recently lost a relative to gun violence.

His death was shown on the TV news. At the time, I didn't know I would soon see eight more of my family and friends named as victims on the screen, but I already had that strange emptiness of mourning. I hated news programs. So I never watched, but that day in November I felt something strange. I kept going through the channels in search of something to watch. Then I found a father holding a necklace just like mine.

"This little necklace was on his neck. The only thing my son had, other than his clothes, was this necklace. Then, they (the policemen) said my son had a gun. Is this a gun? Does this kill someone?"

AISHA
PAZ

It was Sidnei, Jardel's father. One of the seven teenagers who were murdered that night, along with several adults. Jardel liked soccer, being with friends, and had a necklace exactly like mine. Although I didn't know him, at the time the only thing I could think about was that it could have been me. It would be me if I'd been there. And I felt like everything around me was falling apart.

I think this is the most important moment in someone's life: when the person realizes that certain violence is systematized. And to the system, they are not real persons, they are numbers. The violence is not because of what they did, but because of who they are. For their color, for their address, for their economic status. It is the genocide of an entire race through imprisonment and marginalization. My race. I could only ask, "How could I have been a conformist about the death of my people for so long?"—and that was how that conformism and that passivity ended.

I wanted to be seen, heard, and wanted them to respect

my NO. Our no. I wanted them to stop. With over a hundred other people, I laid on the floor and shouted, "Why did you shoot me?" in front of the police. I wasn't just acting. It was how I felt. How those families, friends, neighbors, and supporters felt. It was the weight of all the shots I'd carried with me, accumulated for thirteen years. As if there was something stuck in my throat that prevented me from breathing. I was tired of being ignored. I wanted them to know that I existed and wanted to continue existing.

THE ROLE OF PROTESTS

Sidnei said he wanted his son's death to change society. I don't know if he has succeeded as of today, because I am unable to measure, but he has changed me. The death of the eleven has echoed around every corner and alley. Their pain went beyond a simple television screen and has been embedded in our hearts. The marches followed both in the favelas where the victims lived and in the city center. They killed boys dancing on the sidewalk and men going out to buy cigarettes, with no criminal records, and they still had the courage to complain when we blocked large urban centers with our posters. It was like they were saying "Okay, I know it's wrong but it's over. Shut up."

I couldn't shut up. Not anymore. And I was not the only one. Then, the real protests started. Not only in Curió, but more than ten neighborhoods started to actively protest. Tires were burnt. Traffic was paralyzed on several major avenues. We cried for justice until the forty-four policemen were charged. Today, almost five years later, ten have been acquitted for "lack of evidence" and the rest remain free with Black blood on their hands. Every year in November, we march for justice. For the eleven

208

and millions of others around the world. We speak their names out loud to immortalize them in our verses. My people were marginalized. They chose to put us aside. They decided which color and which social class would suffer. They decided who would die.

Alisson. Jardel. Álef. Renayson. Patricio. Jandson. Francisco. Valmir. Pedro. Marcelo da Silva. Marcelo Pereira. Present!

EMPATHY

In 2020, I had the opportunity to go to the United States. It was the first time I left my country. Some of my biggest inspirations came from the American territory I was stepping on. Angela Davis, Martin Luther King, Jr., Margaret Hamilton, Malcolm X, Katherine Johnson . . . Being in the United States was a journey in myself and in the values that I preached. My host family was white, had two beautiful daughters and two giant dogs. As far away as possible from my reality as a Black girl from a low-income family, with too many people in a small house to adopt dogs. I remember sleeping on the couch there because the idea of having a bed just for me was too strange.

Having a totally different lifestyle made me question a lot of my ideas about the world. Purchasing power, possession of weapons, the effects of segregation in society, war, peace, military enlistment, diplomatic missions, Latin identity . . . it was a lot to process. Some ideas were reinforced, others became a blank space. Getting out of your comfort zone definitely makes you reflect. I have suffered prejudice all my life. As a woman. As a Black person. As a

AISHA
PAZ

"Latina." I thought I'd done enough to support humanity but, unintentionally, it was so common to fight mostly for the causes I relate to and forget about supporting other causes. I ended up being passive about other people's pain because I was too worried about my own issues. Even knowing so much, I knew nothing. We all do. Being there reminded me of it.

Militancy is not fighting for what is best for you, but through your experience with pain, understanding the pain of others and supporting them. There is no ruler to measure just how much each oppressed group suffers, so there is no real way to say that one suffers more than the other. There is so much mutual understanding that some groups have shown support for others in their own efforts and even given up talking about their own issues to prioritize certain issues of other causes needing visibility. In June, it was Pride Month, but since society was still being impacted by events related to Black Lives Matter, some of the organizers gave their visibility to the Black community. You can often see the mutual respect between people and the causes behind them.

THE ROLE OF PROTESTS

HEALING

On a very cold day—in fact, the worst temperatures I had ever faced as a resident of a tropical country—I participated in Martin Luther King, Jr. Day in Raleigh, North Carolina. During the visit to his monument in Washington, DC, I felt filled with strength, but when I was walking in the street with another hundred people it was like I found my place. Not only because it was warmer than on the sidewalk. It was because I felt safe, understood, and respected by those around me. And suddenly I wanted to scream.

I wanted to scream until my voice ended. I wanted to scream until my lungs ran out of air. I wanted to scream like the day I laid on the floor for the deaths in Curió. I wanted to spit that thing out of my throat, because for the first time it looked like it was going to come out. I heard the choir sing for the freedom of all people, and I cried the entire way as I held up posters for the stone of hope. It was at the age of seventeen in a foreign country, surrounded by strangers, that I understood the real meaning of the protests and marches.

AISHA
PAZ

Before, I had a vision that protests and marches were to show indignation. Indignation for injustice, for postmodern slavery, for social inequality, for gender-based violence, for the neglect of the state, for the bad treatment of immigrants... And I was not entirely wrong. What I didn't know about marches and protests is that they are also a way of relieving the pain of those who suffer. We are there to celebrate mothers who cry for their children, to strengthen injured bodies, to relieve wounds. We are there to mend the fragile hearts that are so weakened by the sad ruptures made by humanity's mistakes. You can only understand what happens in a protest, a march, a tribute, when you understand the reason why it's happening. That is why it is so necessary that you seek to know.

How could you understand my behavior if you didn't know my story? If I hadn't told you all this, what would you think of the girl who burns tires? How can you say this is not fair? How can you say it is not necessary? Who are you to measure pain that you don't know?

MOVING FORWARD

Being there in Curió made a difference for me. It didn't solve the problem. I couldn't bring the dead back. Any of them. And I wanted to. I want to play with my cousins, I want to chat late on the street, I want to wear whatever I like without fear, I want to have a bed in my room, I want to eat without thinking about those who don't, I want to swim in a sea without plastic. But it never depended solely on me or those who walked with me on the streets. If the changes depended only on those who believe it would be easy. This has always depended on those who do not participate. Educate yourself, spread your knowledge, question your privileges, don't compromise with unfair attitudes, correct people, be corrected. We need to take a step back and act as if our existence depends on the existence of others. Because it does. In the end, claiming justice is not just the duty of those directly affected, but of everyone who agrees with justice. We cannot be passive about what's wrong. We cannot be ignorant. We cannot accept bad apples. Anywhere. Everywhere. When we find bad apples, we must throw them away.

Aisha Paz is seventeen years old and lives in Fortaleza, Brazil. Even knowing violence at an early age, she believes that happiness is a warm gun. Aisha is a Youth Ambassador 2020 and founded a Non-Governmental Organization (NGO) called De Mãos Dadas that fights for gender equality. She currently sells her art and tries to change the world for the better.

AN ALLY'S MANIFESTO 17

JOEL LEON

I F YOU WERE EXCITED to watch *The Help* upon its release, you were not alone. The film grossed $216.6 million U.S. domestically. What about *Green Book?* $327.9 million. There is nothing America loves more than white heroism, specifically white heroism flavored with a dash of a struggling Black person in need of a white hero in order to achieve their goal. However, the fantasy of white allyship tends to occur more often in the movies than in reality. There is an inaccessible form of martyrdom that has become attractive to those who are seeking to absolve themselves from the pangs of having to deal with America's often ignored history. It's the complicit history of whiteness that has played itself out as the constant drum beat against the screams and cries of Black lives lost.

And so, we have seen self-proclaimed allies yell from the top of their mountainous soap boxes that they, too, have bled, have the Blackest of friends, know all the words to any song currently playing on Hot 97, all of the dance moves and rituals, and have been invited to any and all picnics; have marched, been beaten, and bear the scars to prove themselves worthy. These same allies maybe even voted for Obama. It is this kind of surface level allyship, while admirable, that can often leave those on the sidelines wondering: Is your care for the community or your ego? Amy Cooper, a lifelong Democrat, weaponized her whiteness against Christian Cooper in a way that clearly demonstrates just how performative allyship can be not only dangerous, but potentially deadly.

True allyship requires a deep conditioned deprogramming, a total dismantling of the praxis that is white supremacy and all its oppressive glory. It requires an ever-evolving introspection into the relationships created, the language used; the positions, thoughts, and beliefs held; and how privilege upholds them and at the same time protects the ego from doing the work of detaching itself from all the ways whiteness benefits from keeping the marginalized, marginalized. Until there is a real conversation with white people amongst white people about how they benefit from their whiteness, Hollywood will continue to profit off the white savior complex and the prevailing racial tropes that make allyship a placebo of faux moral support for a cause and movement; an easy way to show up when needed, as needed, to either remain violently silent or aggressively convicted when Blackness and the deaths of Black bodies are no longer media news fodder or a screenwriter's playground. Our moral compass can easily become just another form of blanket protest if our hearts are not truly invested in Black liberation, outside of what is popular and trendy at the moment.

The Black community has allowed you into their homes. We have shown you—given you culture, cooked your meals, swept your floors, raised your children, and fought in your wars. We have built this country with our hands, blood-soaked fingers tinkering with machines and sweat-drenched bodies toiling in fields, cut by noose, whip, and cotton bale. We have marched for liberty, died for freedom; and sat at counters for food, for justice, for equal water fountain access. We have born you music, art, literature—painted pictures, shared and told stories, tales of freedom marchers, freedom fighters, and revolutionaries galore. All for the opportunity to be free, to be equal.

This is why the demand for allyship is no longer table stakes. It's because of this, we do not ask, we demand for allies in this resistance. This moment in our nation is a pivotal one, unlike any we have seen since the Civil Rights Movement of the Sixties. A Monmouth University poll found that seventy-six percent of Americans (seventy-one percent of white people) called racism and discrimination "a big problem" in the country. In June, *The New York Times* reported that since the killing of George Floyd, American voters' support for the Black Lives Matter movement increased almost as much as it had in the preceding

JOEL
LEON

two years. Solidarity is as high as it's ever been since the Ferguson uprisings following the murder of Mike Brown five years ago.

But, if there is anything we are learning through the growth of this movement, throughout this process of healing and dismantling the systems we are re-imagining for ourselves, it is that there can be no safety nets in allyship. Being an "ally" does not mean showing up only when it is convenient or easy. Allyship does not come in waves. It is an ethos, a value system, in which bigger and broader ideas on how to end systemic racism, sexism, gender, age, and disability bias are key to true liberation for all.

Allyship defies convenience. It means support that lives beyond only those who meet your quality standards. True allyship does not exist if your attempts of support for marginalized communities only come on the condition that they do not jeopardize your privilege and security. All of the book clubs joined and movies watched do not a good ally make. If the activism is not put into practice, at best it becomes the foundation for a lack of true substance within movement spaces.

If we are not mindful of the intention behind the work, being an ally can be performative art, a carefully constructed tap-dance, tiptoeing on the tightrope of white and Persons of Color savior-ism. For those not fully invested in learning how to show up not just as allies, but as real-time accomplices in the movement for the Black community, the work can feel more like a ploy to be visible rather than a sustainable effort towards liberation. Performative allyship and movement activism can invalidate the work that has been happening before this moment in time. Please know, there have been folx showing up and doing the work in the streets and in the tweets long before it became trendy or an opportunity to guilt people into showing up for the cause. We each have our calling. And we each have to create space for one another to show up. But let's remember that the wane in enthusiasm we may see is not a reflection of the work required to decolonize, not just these physically oppressive systems, but our hearts. It is merely a part of what happens when folx become unsure of how to sustain mobility within a movement. That is where allyship becomes a substantial part in this work of liberation.

Being a good ally does not get you brownie points, brownies, or a jar of medals. Being a good ally does not afford you special accommodations at your favorite sports club or local sporting event; no free tickets to parades; no discounts on meals or special stays at any boutique hotel in a gentrified neighborhood. There is no special caravan of floats, minstrel puppets, no Olympics, no stolen conspiracy fireworks, or celebratory dynamite to blow up project buildings for gentrification purposes only. The work of allyship does not include banner ads, paid campaigns, post analytics, or an influencer partnership proclaiming Black Lives Matter for a t-shirt and a cocktail kit courtesy of good Black folx everywhere and an Instagram story. Your allyship is not makeup, a makeover, or a makeshift way of bleeding out your failures as a human who has used their lack of Blackness to shield you from conflict, from challenges, and questions about your allyship from Black and non-POC persons. Allyship is bigger than a two-party system, and cannot be steeped in guilt, in shame, in approval; it cannot be coated in favor, an opportunity to save yourself or rid yourself of the embarrassment of being late to the "save a Black life" party.

The allyship I speak of may opt to put its body on the line but its spirit always chooses to live within the cross hairs of social justice. It means making a conscious decision that freedom is greater than fear; that dismantling the systems that destroy us matters more than upholding our egos. Allyship means understanding our own prejudices, our biases, and even some of our own racist projections in order to not just get to a place of unpacking, but one of existential reform and transcendent healing of all beliefs that cling to white supremacy. It is not enough to simply protest or have the hard conversations with those around you, but to serve as an ally also requires that you take a look in the mirror that is more receptive and expansive than the deflection and defensiveness that keep us from scrutinizing our inner truths. I've seen the most noted of allies who easily tout how much and how often they have stood up against injustices, turn a blind eye when those same injustices hit too close to home. This is why many in the social justice community have turned to the word "accomplice" rather than ally. Accomplice speaks to an individual who sacrifices the same level of physical and spiritual safety for the sake of being truly complicit in dismantling the systems that oppress us all.

Allyship is not just about signing petitions; yes, this is part of the progressive movement towards liberation, just as protesting, marching, boycotting, and learning and relearning are. True allyship is a lived-in ethos that governs how we see, think, and embrace the world around us. It lives in the same space as abolition, as anti-racism—a theory that is a lifelong practice that enables us to reframe how we show up for social movements. Allyship gets to be bigger than the moment at hand because it has to be, needs to be, for a reimagined future to occur. It is a choice driven by compassion, by empathy, and a solidarity that extends beyond Breonna Taylor, beyond Philando Castillo, beyond George Floyd, Ahmaud Arbery, Tamir Rice, and Sandra Bland. It is a choice that must be made every day, a choice that demands our full attention and our deepest intentions. It is a choice that calls us to be proactive not neutral; a choice that requires us to take actions that live outside of just the mail of a petition, the feet in a protest.

JOEL LEON

It is a choice that means looking inwardly, deeply. It calls us to be present in the moments when we see or hear racist behaviors in our space. We are being asked to be braver than we have been expected to be. It is a choice that asks of us to question our own behaviors and the behaviors of those closest to us—the ways in which we think, act, and are in the world. A choice that recognizes the need for empathetic and engaged efforts of confrontation, of challenging whatever has existed that has allowed systems of oppression to progress and sit neatly in our daily lives. It is indeed the opposite of peaceful or pacifist. An ally is an active participant in decolonization, a system that is very much active in its role to police and murder Black bodies does not need docility. It requires frank conversations and aggressive protocol. It requires all of us, including allies, to be braver, bolder, and more belligerent in our quest for freedom, by and all means necessary.

To all of our allies, young and old, Black, Brown, trans, queer, able-bodied, differently abled, and those living with a disability seen or unseen, this is our fight. There is no science to making a good ally. The work of allyship will have to live outside of your "self" to be progressive enough to shift the balance of power that continues to destroy our present day. If we all are to be free, then we all need to be allies in support of the liberation of us all. Allyship is a verb, it is active. Allyship is a verbal, physical, and spiritual contract that says, "everything that ails or harms another also ails or harms me." It is empathy on steroids. It is living beyond your own needs, comfort, your potential misgivings, and recognizing that liberation is an all-or-nothing venture. And that allyship is not just for white citizens of the world. Allyship speaks to all persons with privileges who live outside of the spectrum, to those who have advantages in other areas and are willing to not only do the work with their words, but with their hearts and minds attached to the effort. Allyship is not a balm, but the glue that both bonds and builds us as a collective, as a community, and as a people.

Let's get free. Let's get active. Let us all be the allies we need to be.

Joel Leon (Joel L. Daniels) is a performer, author and storyteller who writes and tells stories for Black people. A Bronx native, Joel has collaborated with The Gates Foundation and HBO, and has appeared on NBC's *TODAY*, *Insider*, and Sirius XM. His writing has been featured in *Forbes*, *Newsweek.com*, the *Huffington Post*, *Blavity*, *BBC News*, and *Medium*. His recent TED Talk on healthy coparenting has been viewed over 1.2 million times globally, and he is the author of *Book About Things I Will Tell My Daughter* and *God Wears Durags, Too.*

OUR HUMAN FAMILY

THE ONLINE PUBLICATION, OUR HUMAN FAMILY, has been fostering conversations about achieving equality since April 2019. Our goal is to unite the world—our world, our sphere of influence—by dispelling the lie of race and the practice of racism and replacing them with the truth of love and equality.

If you have been enlightened or inspired by our writers' works, intended to broaden perspectives and foster meaningful conversations, then your continued membership to *Medium.com* will provide unlimited access to the outstanding narratives we publish.

Our Human Family, Inc. is now a 501(c)(3) charitable organization, with the same goals and message as the online Our Human Family publication. Still in its early planning stages, Our Human Family, Inc. advocates for racial equality and inclusion in America by creating and offering workshops, panel discussion groups, targeting key educational programs for sponsorship, hosting guest speaker events, and much more that will help us achieve racial equality and inclusion for everyone.

We understand that there is no one-size-fits-all approach to people. The same applies to providing the various segments of our customer base with the knowledge and skills necessary to eradicate racism. We make this possible by creating informative and transformative materials that will evolve with the times and meet the specific needs of various segments of our consumer base.

The subject of racism is broad and complicated. Its components required close examination and nuanced explanation. While our message is singular, we must tailor our conversations and presentations to bring awareness to these aspects. These items must also be updated to reflect the challenges of the times.

We cannot do the work of equality without the support of people like you. In the same way that it takes a village to raise a child, it will take all of us to end racism and create a more equitable world. Our Human Family, Inc. is working to bring an end to racism and establish a society rooted in equality. You can help us continue our anti-racism work.

Please support the critical work and word of Our Human Family at the forefront of the national conversation on better race relations and widespread equality in America by making a donation at *ourhumanfamily.org/ contribute.*

Love one another.

CONNECT WITH US

OURHUMANFAMILY.ORG

FACEBOOK.COM/OURHUMANFAM

INSTAGRAM.COM/OURHUMANFAM

MEDIUM.COM/OUR-HUMAN-FAMILY

TWITTER.COM/OURHUMANFAM

INFO@OURHUMANFAMILY.ORG

OURHUMANFAMILY.ORG/GIVING

ALSO FROM OUR HUMAN FAMILY

We are pleased to announce selected works by James Baldwin will serve as the inspiration for the upcoming *OHF Magazine*, Issue 2 Fall/Winter 2020. The issue goes on sale December 2020 at ourhumanfamily.org.

LOVE ONE ANOTHER.

Made in the USA
Coppell, TX
07 October 2020

39450460R10163